JESUS IN THE SYNOPTIC GOSPELS

Jᴇsus ɪɴ ᴛʜᴇ Sʏɴᴏᴘᴛɪᴄ Gᴏsᴘᴇʟs is one of the volumes in the series, IMPACT BOOKS, designed to bring the modern reader the significant achievements of scholars, both Catholic and non-Catholic, in the fields of Scripture, Theology, Philosophy, Mathematics, History, and the Physical and Social Sciences. Among the titles in the series are:

Jesus
in the Synoptic Gospels

by WILLIAM E. LYNCH, C.M.

THE BRUCE PUBLISHING COMPANY / MILWAUKEE

IMPRIMI POTEST:
James A. Fischer, C.M.
Provincial

NIHIL OBSTAT:
Richard J. Sklba, S.S.L., S.T.D.
Censor deputatus

IMPRIMATUR:
✠ William E. Cousins
Archbishop of Milwaukee
June 5, 1967

Library of Congress Catalog Card Number: 67–26340

© 1967 William E. Lynch, C.M.
MADE IN THE UNITED STATES OF AMERICA

Preface

It is an exciting challenge to attempt to explain the writings of Matthew, Mark, and Luke. There are many reasons for this challenge. First, the Christian reader comes to the Gospels with a good basic knowledge of Jesus Christ. What can be added? Second, the Gospels are not meant to be studied as much as to be lived. Why explain life? Is life not rather to be experienced? Third, and most important, the object of the writings of Matthew, Mark, and Luke is Jesus of Nazareth, the incarnate Word — a mystery in himself.

I have tried to meet this challenge by offering some of the insights into the Gospels which current biblical scholars have been able to make. I believe that these insights will be of help to the man of Christian faith in experiencing Christ and in identifying himself with Jesus. In the following pages I have provided (1) an introduction to each of the Synoptic Gospels, (2) a detailed exegesis of a few passages from each of the Synoptic evangelists, and (3) a hopefully judicious repetition of the most fundamental notions of contemporary New Testament scholarship.

Before we can begin our investigation of each of the Synoptic Gospels, it is important to have clearly in mind what a commentary on the Gospels is. Therefore some prefatory remarks are in order, and I hope that these will give the reader an initial insight into what the Gospels are and will likewise show him the scope and limitations of the present volume.

Contemporary biblical scholars distinguish three basic levels of tradition in the Gospels. The first is the life and words of

Jesus of Nazareth, son of God. The second is the early Church's understanding, consolidation, and development of Jesus' deeds and teachings. The final stratum of tradition is the understanding and use of Christ's life and words by each Gospel's author. This conclusion of modern scholarship is reflected in the *Dogmatic Constitution on Divine Revelation* promulgated by the Fathers of Vatican II. In this document we read:

> Holy Mother Church has firmly and with absolute constancy held, and continues to hold, that the four Gospels . . . whose historical character the Church unhesitatingly asserts, faithfully hand on what Jesus Christ, while living among men, really did and taught for their eternal salvation until the day He was taken up into heaven. . . . Indeed, after the ascension of the Lord the apostles handed on to their hearers what he had said and done. This they did with that clearer understanding which they enjoyed after they had been instructed by the events of Christ's risen life and taught by the light of the Spirit of truth. The sacred authors wrote the four Gospels, selecting some things from the many which had been handed on by word of mouth or in writing, reducing some of them to a synthesis, explicating some things in view of the situation of their Churches, and preserving the form of proclamation but always in such fashion that they told us the honest truth about Jesus. For their intention in writing was that either from their own memory and recollections, or from the witness of those who themselves "from the beginning were eyewitnesses and ministers of the word" we might know the "truth" concerning those matters about which we have been instructed (cf. Lk 1:2–4) (par. 19).

To see what this means, let us take up each of the three levels.

1. The first level: Christ's words and life. Of the first thirty years of the life of Jesus, little is told in the Gospels. Of his words during that period, perhaps only one sentence is known. With the *history* of these years as well as the remaining short span of Jesus' life, this commentary is not concerned. Later in this preface we shall delve more deeply into this historical query.

2. The second level: the early Church's transmission of the life and words of Christ. More than thirty years passed after the resurrection and the writing of the Gospel according to Mark, the earliest Gospel we now possess. During that lengthy period, the Church looked deeply into the life and words of its Lord. The most immediate need of the first Christians was to explain the death of the one they claimed as God's beloved in a unique way. From this need arose the passion narratives, which explain that God had foreordained the death of his beloved Son. These passion narratives, which constitute a major portion of our written Gospels, were thus originally early apologetic efforts by the apostolic Church.

The first Christians also wished to spread their own joy in the "good news" that is Jesus. They developed a somewhat stereotyped method of preaching or of proclaiming the message of salvation of Jesus — this is the kerygma of which we hear so much today. An instance of the kerygma as announced to the Jews is found in the speech of Peter to the community at Jerusalem:

> Jesus of Nazareth was a man accredited to you by God through miracles and wonders and signs, which God did through him in your midst, as you yourselves know. When he was delivered up by the settled purpose and foreknowledge of God, you crucified and slew him by the hands of wicked men. But God has raised him up, having put an end to the pangs of death, because it was not possible that death should hold him. . . . Have a change of heart and mind . . . and be baptized every one of you in the name of Jesus Christ for the remission of your sins; then you will receive the gift of the Holy Spirit (Acts 2:22–24, 38).

Similar instances of this early kerygmatic proclamation of the saving Christ are found in Acts 3:12–26; 10:37–43; 13:23–41.

In addition, the early followers of Jesus prayed together and soon wrote hymns (Eph 5:16; 1 Tim 3:16; Phil 2:5–11; Col 1:16 f.) and fitting prayers; for instance, the two forms of the Lord's Prayer in Mt 6:9 ff. and Lk 11:2–4.

They also wished to remember Jesus' teaching on many points; for example, marriage, fasting, attitude toward sinners, the place of love. Therefore the Church developed capsulized formulas of his sayings: "What God has yoked together, man may not separate" (Mk 10:9); "Can wedding guests fast as long as the bridegroom is with them?" (Mk 2:19); "It is my mission to call sinners and not saints" (Mk 2:17); "Love your neighbor as yourself" (Mt 22:39). In fact, we could divide almost all of the first three Gospels into sayings, miracle stories, parables, the passion narrative, and a few other categories. The early Church needed such accounts to spread its understanding of Christ.

From all this, it should be evident that the needs of the early Church influenced its transmission of the good news. The social milieu and religious concepts of the first century affected the early Church's understanding of Jesus' life and words. Part and parcel of a Roman-dominated Palestine, the first disciples thought as Jews of their day and age.

The second level of tradition found within the Gospels is very important for understanding what the Gospels are, but it is not the precise object of the explanations found in this volume. An investigation into this second level of tradition more properly provides subject matter for a study of the *formation* of the Gospels, of their development from the kerygmatic preaching of the early Church, and the subsequent instruction into the meaning of the Christian life.

3. The third level: the Gospels' development of Christ's life and words. It would seem that the words of Christ could be lost to tradition with the progression of time and the development of the interpretation of his words. No one will deny this possibility. Does this mean, therefore, that the Gospels are not God's own words?

As Christians, we believe that God did move the responsible agents of the Bible to write faithfully what he wanted written. The result is that the whole Bible is God's word. While, therefore, the Gospels may contain few of the very words of Christ, we believers see them as God's written word. And the Gospels as inspired by God are the object of the explanations of this book.

To understand the Gospels as inspired, we must understand the human author, his purpose, and those to whom he wrote. Introductions to each Gospel will explain these principles for each evangelist.

Scholars who have intensely investigated the sources of the first three Gospels for more than 150 years have coined a name for the problem, calling it the "Synoptic Question." The name "synoptic" etymologically means "to look together." The Synoptic Gospels, Matthew, Mark, and Luke, unlike John, give a kind of synopsis of Christ's life and words. The "Synoptic Problem" or "Question" seeks to ascertain the sources of the first three Gospels which resulted in their synopsis and similarity in content and form.

We would be presumptuous to do more than mention the problem here. Scholars are still unresolved on the solution. The facts are: (1) an early tradition favoring an Aramaic Matthew; (2) 330 verses of the first three Gospels are so identical as to require common written source(s), not merely oral sources; (3) all but 50 verses of Mk are in Mt; (4) Mt has about 330 verses not found in Mk or Lk; (5) Lk has about 550 verses not found in the other two.

A fairly widely accepted explanation of these five facts is the following: (1) Mk's sources were mainly oral traditions. (2) Mt and Lk used: (a) Mark's Gospel; (b) a Greek translation of an Aramaic work (Matthew's Aramaic — ?) containing sayings and deeds (?) of Jesus, called Q (from German *Quelle*, meaning source); (c) and variant oral and other written traditions. The contents and structure of the hypothesized Q are disputed among scholars.

It would be of some value to know the answer to the Synoptic Question, but its importance should not be exaggerated. Of importance for our treatment will be the presumption that Mt and Lk depend on Mk.

Brief review of principles of interpretation. In order to appreciate the vision of Jesus provided by each of the Synoptic evangelists, it is necessary to have some grasp of the general principles used in interpreting the Bible. Therefore we shall briefly summarize them here.

In interpreting the evangelical use of the early Church's traditions about the life and words of Jesus, an understanding of the author, audience, and sources of the Gospel is required. In addition, we must also know the meaning of a particular word, both in itself, in a particular Gospel, and in the special context in which it is used. The phrase, "The measure you use in measuring will be used to measure out your share" has different meanings in Lk 6:38 and in Mk 4:24. In Mark's Gospel the context surrounding the saying requires it to have a meaning somewhat as follows: "Listen attentively and do something about God's parabolic word." The context in Lk, on the other hand, demands us to understand it in terms of generosity and of not judging.

Another and highly important principle of interpretation hinges on the literary form of a Gospel message. It makes quite a difference whether we consider "I must be frank with you: if one is not born anew, he cannot see the kingdom of God" (Jn 3:5) as a literal, historical fact or as some sort of figure. As an historical fact, it would be teaching that a man must crawl back into his mother's womb!

This rapid review of the principles of interpretation gives some idea of the problems facing biblical scholars. Little wonder that they often disagree in the interpretation of the *literal* sense of the Gospels, i.e., that meaning intended by both God and the human author, what we can term the sense *of* the Bible. The Church has the right to determine this sense, so we believe, but only a dozen texts in the entire Bible have been given an official interpretation by the Church, and most of these have to do with the sacraments. Hence there is considerable freedom in determining the literal sense of a particular passage. In addition to the literal sense, there are three other important "senses" of Scripture which scholars have distinguished. We might sum up their conclusions by saying that there are, in addition to the literal sense: (1) a *fuller* or *typical* sense — the sense *in* the Bible — that meaning meant by God alone; (2) a *theological* sense or sense *out* of the Bible, that meaning which theologians draw from an inspired passage by relating it to nonrevealed, humanly known truths; and (3) an *accommodated* sense or sense *into* the Bible, that meaning placed upon a text by, for example, a preacher. In our study we will be concerned exclusively with the

literal sense intended both by God and by the human authors
of the Gospels.

At the beginning of our investigation into each of the Synoptic
Gospels we shall offer some principles for understanding them.
These principles are the most important part of this book. With
their help you can grapple with the meaning of Gospel passages
not examined in detail in the present volume.

The Gospels as history. After considering the three levels of
tradition and the rules for interpreting the Bible, we must pay
special attention to the knotty problem of the Gospels as history.

What is history? We of a Greco-Roman culture look on history
as "a thing that happened." No one would seriously suggest that
everything narrated in the Gospels actually happened. Was there
ever a good Samaritan, a particular net catching good and bad
fish, our Lord acting as a shepherd to be the "Good Shepherd"?
But to question whether there was a Jesus of Nazareth, or if he
died or rose, endangers the very bases of Christianity, which has
always claimed to be a religion in which time and eternity melded
in the one sent from God to be our redeemer.

We do not, however, propose to answer the question of the
historicity of the Gospels. Here we are looking at the Gospels
as God's word, as particular books written for their own purpose
and audience. One of the very least important purposes of the
Gospels was to lay down "a thing that happened." At times, and
this will be noted in the commentary, the literary form of a
particular section will be "a thing that happened," a statistic.
For more details of the Gospels as history, we think the reader
should turn to a New Testament history, to apologetics, or to
books about the quest for the historical Jesus.

Summary. The Gospels, as we now have them, are the result
of three steps of development: first, the life and words of Jesus
of Nazareth; second, thirty years of understanding of his life
and words by the Church; and third, the evangelists' own inspired teaching about his life and words. This book will treat
only the final level: Matthew's, Mark's, and Luke's inspired
interpretation of Jesus' life and teachings.

The challenge raised by any effort to interpret the Gospels clearly sounds: "What did Matthew, Mark, and Luke mean by a particular verse written to the people meant to be their readers?" For helping us accept the challenge, we are most grateful to many authors, teachers, and associates, especially Mrs. Genevieve Huxoll. The Kleist-Lilly translation of the New Testament is used throughout this work, except where noted. The shortcomings of the book, of course, must be attributed to its author. He prays that no one who studies it will be hindered in his approach to God's word through Matthew, Mark, and Luke about Jesus of Nazareth, God's only Son.

Contents

JESUS IN THE SYNOPTIC GOSPELS

CHAPTER ONE

Jesus in the Gospel According to Mark

Historical background. There are two "proofs" or "indications" that Mark wrote the "second" Gospel. The first is that of external witnesses. Papias (ca. A.D. 130), Justin (ca. A.D. 150), Irenaeus (ca. A.D. 200), Tertullian (ca. A.D. 225), Clement of Alexandria (d. A.D. 215), and other early Christian writers attest that Mark was Peter's disciple or "interpreter" and that it was Mark who composed the second Gospel. For instance, Papias, who was bishop of Hierapolis in Phrygia and a disciple of the "presbyter" (identified by many with John the apostle), records in his *Explanations of the Sayings of the Lord* that Mark was Peter's "Interpreter" and that he "wrote down carefully, though not in order, all that he remembered, both words and deeds, of the Lord." Irenaeus tells us that Mark left us "Peter's preaching in writing," and Tertullian says that his Gospel could well be called the Gospel of Peter.

There are, in addition, internal indications within the Gospel according to Mark that its author was associated with Peter. Mark's Gospel follows, for one thing, the oral preaching or kerygmatic proclamation of Peter, as is evident if one compares the structure of Mark's Gospel with the preaching of Peter found

1

in Acts, particularly in Acts 10:34–43. Second, the vivid details of the Gospel indicate that it is based on an eyewitness report. His account of Jesus' deeds is more lively and popular than those found in Mt and Lk. Only Mk, for example, gives the name of the blind man and relates that Jesus gave the name "sons of thunder" to the sons of Zebedee. In addition, Peter plays a prominent role in the Gospel (in 1:36 the disciples are called "Simon and they that were with him"). Finally, there are more Latinisms in Mk than in any other Gospel. This accords well with the tradition that Mark wrote it in Rome, where he had gone with Peter.

Who was this Mark? Very likely, he was the "John Mark" referred to in Acts 13:5–13; 15:36–41; 1 Pet 5:13; Col 4:10; and other passages of the New Testament. If we grant that Mark the evangelist and John Mark are the same person, then we know that he was a Jew of Jerusalem who spoke Greek as well as Aramaic. Mark's psychological outlook, as learned from the Gospel, was that of a youth, full of vigor, hardly able to contain his message.

What was the audience for whom Mark wrote his Gospel? He wrote for Gentile Christians, not for a Jewish-Christian community. We know this because Mark, unlike Matthew, finds it necessary to explain Jewish customs and practices, such as ablutions before meals and washing of vessels, the Parasceve, the Day of Preparation, etc. He regularly translates Aramaic words and phrases which would have been unintelligible to Greek-speaking Gentile Christian communities. Most likely, he composed his Gospel for the Gentile community in Rome, although this cannot be shown to be absolutely true.

Although it is not possible to determine conclusively when the Gospel of Mark was written, it is highly probable that it was composed after the death of Peter and before the destruction of Jerusalem in A.D. 70. Tradition is not unanimous about its date: Irenaeus and an ancient prologue to the Gospel explicitly affirm that it was written after Peter's death, whereas Clement of Alexandria maintains that it was written while Peter was still alive. The testimony of Papias, which is the earliest witness to the Gospel, accords better with the tradition of Irenaeus. For this and other reasons most contemporary scholars date the Gospel between A.D. 65–70.

Of the three Synoptic Gospels, Mk is perhaps most important for its very primitive portrayal of the humanity of Jesus. We shall see this as we examine in detail some representative passages from the Gospel.

Literary forms and style of Mark. The "gospel" itself may be considered a literary form. As such, a gospel is the grouping of pre-existing stories, such stories as have been noted in the preface, e.g., pronouncement stories, miracle stories, the passion narrative, parables, etc. Mark put these pre-existing stories together, frequently by adding *and's*. There is a certain amount of originality in Mark, but he is much more a composing redactor than an author. His style is unrefined, although he has an eye for plot and contrast.

Outline. Mark admits of no easy general divisions. Some scholars, following the early Church's kerygma, divide this Gospel into two major parts 1–8:30 and 8:31–16:8. 1–8:30 give Jesus' public life and miracles, and culminate in Peter's confession. The second part, 8:31–16:8, tells the suffering and death of Jesus.

We prefer the following outline. It is quite detailed and gives an overall view of Mark's teachings. This general view is essential for an understanding of all and any part of Mk. The outline is also meant to afford a reference for further study of sections which are not treated here.

FIRST PART. The Introduction. Mark teaches that God witnessed to Jesus' final mission (1:1–13).

I. The joyful tidings of the divine Jesus, Messiah (1:1).

II. Prologue. The Old Testament's foretold eschatological times have begun (1:2–8).

III. Time and eternity meld in a divine man (1:9–11).

IV. The first act of the mission of God's Son: to be attacked by the devil (1:12 f.).

SECOND PART. The good news of the kingdom of God is preached (1:14–8:26).
  I. God's message through Jesus: repentance and confidence (1:14 f.).
 II. Jesus masterfully calls four lowly fishermen, only promising to make them fishers of men (1:16–20).
III. The first public appearance of our Savior, Jesus Christ (1:21–45).
 IV. A crescendo of conflicts (2:1–3:6).
  V. The height of the Galilean ministry (3:7–6:13).
     A. Summary statement of the external features of Jesus' ministry (3:7–12).
     B. The twelve chosen to accompany Jesus and share his miraculous power (3:13–19).
     C. Jesus' dedicated, detached, and misunderstood holiness; his manifest holy power (3:20–35).
     D. Mark's views on Jesus' "parabolic" teaching and on the kingdom of God (4:1–34).
     E. Wonders about the Sea of Galilee: Jesus, master of wind, sea, demons, and death (4:35–5:43).
     F. Jesus rejected by his overfamiliar countrymen; he can do no miracles for them (6:1–6a).
     G. On a merciful and urgent missionary journey, trust and accept hospitality (6:6b–13).
 VI. The ministry beyond Galilee (6:14–8:26).

THIRD PART. Preparation of the future good news: victory through the passion, death, and resurrection (8:27–13:37).
  I. Suffering for the Messiah and followers; supernatural power (8:27–9:28).
 II. Instructions for disciples: lowliness for the first place; all for Christ; the inestimable value of a soul; holiness (9:29–49).
III. Teaching on adultery, how to enter the kingdom, and on wealth (10:1–31).
 IV. Teachings by stories connected with his final journey to Jerusalem (10:32–52).
     A. Ultimate victory through the passion (10:32–34).
     B. True greatness in sufferings as in the Messiah's example (10:35–45).
     C. A trusting disciple, begging sight, will be given it to follow the Messiah (10:46–52).
  V. The Messiah's activities in Jerusalem (11:1–13:37).
     A. Summary of first three days (11:1–25).
     B. Jesus vanquishes his enemies (11:27–12:44).
     C. Watch — eschatologically motivated warnings (13:1–37).

FOURTH PART. The act of victory (14:1–16:8).
  I. Events culminating in the arrest (14:1–52, cf. below
     under 14:32–42).
 II. Trials, crucifixion, and burial (14:53–15:47).
     A. Trial before the Sanhedrin (14:53–65).
     B. Peter vehemently and cursingly denies Jesus (14:66–
        72).
     C. Jesus' innocence; Jewish guilt, especially the chief
        priests'; Pilate's weakness (15:1–15).
     D. Some mental and physical sufferings of Jesus (15:16–
        20).
     E. Simon impressed to carry Jesus' cross (15:21 f.).
     F. Crucifixion, death, and burial (15:23–47).
III. Reactions to the resurrection: fear or . . . (16:1–8).
     (16:9–20 is an inspired, though spurious, ending.)

Mark's teachings in summary. Mark had much in common
with modern existentialists. Seemingly, he had experienced the
vanity of human existence and of human endeavors. He had gone
through the existential anguish that marks all real quest for life.
Mark found his reason for living in Jesus of Nazareth. For him,
this Jesus was the Messiah, Son of God, and the Man — not
merely as an object of passive belief but as the Person who gave
meaning to Mark's life. Mark had responded and taught others
to respond. Full commitment in loving loyalty was the only road
to the full personality which gives meaning to life. And for
Mark, full personality meant doing God's will, which was death
(for glory).

Mark found a reason for living. Mark's Jesus was, as a Person
sufficient reason for the persecuted and disappointed, for the
shopkeeper and shoplifter, for the sick and failure, for all, to
live. So Mark taught.

Jesus, Son of God (cf. p. 8 ff. on 1:9–11; 6:45–52). Jesus had
divine power. He worked miracles of healing (1:29–31; 1:40–45;
2:1–21). Power over water and over storms was his (4:35–40;
6:45–52). Devils obeyed his rebuke (1:23–26; 1:32–34; 3:20–30;
5:1–20).

Messianic secret. Jesus was also the Messiah. But, Mark
teaches, the true significance of his messianic character was not
perceived while he lived. Time and again, Jesus forbade the

divulging of who he was. The devils (1:34; 3:12), the cured (1:44; 5:43; 7:36; 8:26), the disciples (8:30; 9:9) were forbidden to reveal Jesus as the Christ. Why this caution? Jesus did not want to be misunderstood. The devils and the cured would have broadcast that a wonder-worker, not a savior from sin, had come. The people expected and wanted only a marvel-worker; Jesus came also to save from sin. Even Peter did not properly apprehend the meaning of the messiahship:

> "But you, who do you say I am?" Here Peter spoke up and said to him: "You are the Messiah." . . . Peter drew him aside and proceeded to lecture him. But he turned round and, in sight of his disciples, lectured Peter: "Get out of my sight, Satan!" he said. "You do not take God's view of things, but men's" (8:29, 33).

It is true that Jesus rose, but his manifestation will not come about until the end of time (16:8). The misunderstood Messiah, as we shall see, was a pointed and significant teaching for the misunderstood and persecuted Roman Christians.

Son of Man. This title occurs fourteen times in Mk, and its meaning is disputed. Mark's picture of the perfectly human Jesus (1:9–11; cf. p. 8 ff.(summed up this title of mankind's child, the Son of Man. Mark enthusiastically paints the Man's knowledge, will, and emotions.

Jesus did not know who touched him when the lady with the hemorrhage had been cured (5:30), nor did he know the day of the Last Judgment (13:32). Jesus could not work miracles in Nazareth (6:5).

Mark is equally daring in describing the Man's affections. More than once he sighed deeply (3:5; cf. p. 16; 6:7; 7:34; 8:12). His disciples had to chide, to scold, to admonish him. He slept as they almost drowned (4:33). Peter told Jesus that the Christ would never suffer (8:32). He crossed to the Gerasenes (5:1) only to recross at once after being rejected (5:17–20). He shuddered in terror in Gethsemani (14:33; cf. p. 28 ff.).

It is true that frequently he was merciful and charitable. Compassion brought about the miracle of the loaves and fishes (8:34). Charitably, he ate with public sinners (2:13–17). But Mark also tells that he was frequently angry, grieved, indignant (1:41, Greek text; 3:5; 10:14; cf. p. 25).

Mark's description of the perfectly human Jesus comes out most beautifully in Jesus' tenderness toward children. He insists on food for the twelve-year-old risen girl (5:43). He blesses the children, takes them in his arms, and uses their "gimme" as an example that adults might beg the kingdom (cf. 10:13–16 below). His "woe to their scandalizer" (cf. 9:35 f.; 41) is from a heart filled with love for children.

Man's response. To this human, hidden Messiah, Son of God, man must respond by loving loyalty. The persecuted Romans must, Mark stresses, have active faith. Such faith is opposed both to fear or awe and to sin. Fear or awe makes a man a spectator, not a participant (6:45–52; cf. p. 21). For such, Jesus may be the Son of God — but so what! Sin prevents love. The crass sinner finds hope in Mk. The hypocrite refuses God (2:13–17).

The road to this faith is suffering, which brings knowledge of one's sinfulness. The nothing that is self follows. And then, only then, can a release in an awareness of forgiveness and loyalty be effected. And loyalty requires all that you are, not just for the second, but for every second. Mark tells his readers that:

> It was necessary for the Son of Man to suffer much. . . . If anyone wants to be my follower, he must renounce himself and shoulder his cross: then he may be a follower of mine. Why, he who would save his life shall lose it; but he who freely parts with his life for the sake of the Gospel will save it in the end (cf. 8:31, 34 f.).

Mark can never be the object of abstract study. He invites his readers to life, to the anguish of real living, to adventure, not to security, to a very human Jesus who is life's reason in loyalty — come what suffering may!

These concerns characterize Mark's Gospel. We shall now examine in more detail representative passages from the Gospel of Mark to illustrate in a concrete way what kind of "good news" Mark proclaimed.

TIME AND ETERNITY MELD IN A DIVINE MAN
(Mk 1:9–11)

⁹One day about that time Jesus came from Nazareth in Galilee and had himself baptized by John in the Jordan. ¹⁰As soon as he was coming up out of the water, he saw the heavens opened and the spirit in the shape of a dove descend upon him. ¹¹Moreover, a voice rang out upon the air: "You are my Son, the beloved; with you I am well pleased."

General context. The first part of Mark's Gospel extends from verse 1 to 13 of Chapter 1. It is the introduction to Mark's good news. The book's title, "A summary of the Gospel of Jesus Christ, the Son of God" is given in 1:1. In 1:2–8, Mark teaches that the eschatological or final times promised in the Old Testament have begun. John the Baptist, in fulfillment of the word spoken in Is 40:3 (1:3) had appealed for preparedness (1:4). As Mal 3:1 and 3:23 (Hebrew text numbering of verses) had foretold (1:2), John points to a greater (1:7), whose way he is to prepare by requiring conversion from sin through a symbolic immersion (1:5–8).

We chose 1:9–11 for three reasons. (1) to show Mark's teaching that Jesus is God's Son; (2) to indicate Jesus' mission as Yahweh's servant; and (3) to bring out how human Mark makes the Man.

Literary form. A story about Jesus appears in 1:9–11. By story, we are neither affirming nor denying the historical character of these verses. For other examples of the literary form of "story about Jesus," cf. 1:16–20; 1:35–39; 2:13 f.; 6:1–6a.

Mark's teaching in 1:9–11 can be summed up by saying that God witnesses to Jesus that the Nazarene is his Son. Time and eternity meld in a divine Man.

Exegesis of 1:9–11.

1. (1:9) *One day about that time Jesus came from Nazareth in Galilee and had himself baptized by John in the Jordan.* This verse teaches the paradoxical beginning of the fulfillment proclaimed by John. The man of Nazareth, by coming to be baptized by John, showed his preparedness to do God's will.

This is Mark's first mention of Jesus after the title of the "good news" in 1:1. Jesus was too well known to the early Church to need more introduction than *Jesus came from Nazareth.* Why has Mark, unlike Luke and Matthew, no infancy narrative? Was it lacking in his source material? No one really knows. Any reason suggested is simply an educated guess.

It is of note that Mark, unlike Mathew (3:14 ff.), had no embarrassment in John's baptizing Jesus. The picture of Jesus throughout Mark's Gospel is too primitive for Mark to feel a need to explain. John, too, was a man accredited by God (1:2–4).

A greater difficulty for us, not for Mark, is that Mark connects baptism with the confession of sin; hence, why should Jesus be baptized? "John appeared in the desert to preach a baptism which signified a change of the heart and looked to forgiveness of sins. . . . They confessed their sins and had themselves baptized by him in the Jordan River" (Mk 1:4 f.). Yet Jesus is baptized. Does this mean that Jesus was guilty of sin? Mark sees no problem here, for the question was simply not pertinent at this early period in the Church, when the implications of what it means for a man to be divine were just beginning to be realized. Surely, for Mark, Jesus is divine, nor does Mark predicate sin of Jesus. Nonetheless, Jesus is baptized and John's baptism is connected with sin. Matthew saw the problem and explained it thus: "At that time Jesus arrived from Galilee to meet John at the Jordan and be baptized by him. John tried to stop him" (Mt 3:13). By the time Matthew's Gospel was written the problem of a sinless and divine man had come up. For Mark, Jesus was simply The Man.

Besides, as Mk 1:2–8 shows, Mark saw John's baptism as part of the divine will. How could Jesus not fail to do God's will? Matthew brings the same out more forcefully than Mark: "After all, it is only so that we fulfill as is proper for us, all just demands" (Mt 3:15). Jesus is prepared to do God's will, part of which was a baptism of water in preparation for a baptism of God's spirit: "I baptize you with water; he will baptize you with the holy spirit" (Mk 1:8). The Man from Nazareth chose to do God's will, which was to be baptized by John. A paradoxical fulfillment of John's preaching!

2. (1:10) *As soon as he was coming up out of the water, he saw the heavens opened and the spirit in the shape of a dove descend upon him.* In summary, this verse teaches that Jesus, on emerging from the Jordan and John's baptism, experienced a theophany or encounter with God. In this, the eschatological times, God's power descended to him in an evident form. The power which keeps creation in being is his. There is a new *supercreation.*

a) This verse and the following contain three biblically special occurrences: the heavens' opening, the voice from them, and a man's seeing their opening. Jewish cosmogony divided creation into the earth, the waters below, and the heavens. God dwelt in the heavens; no human saw them opened. The verse thus describes a divine manifestation, that is, a theophany.

Too, the theophany is made in the context of the spirit's descent. The gift of the spirit would be the fulfillment of God's will, as John had promised (1:8) and the Old Testament foretold (Jl 3:1 f.). We are therefore in the beginning of the final ages, the eschatological times when God's gifts and revelation reach their earthly perfection. Mark thereby insinuates that the Nazarene gives meaning to all of the Old Testament and ushers in this final, eschatological age.

b) *The spirit descends.* Is the spirit a person? In the Old Testament the "spirit of Yahweh" is frequent enough. The spirit descends upon judges, kings, and prophets. There is no indication in the entire Old Testament that the spirit is a person. The spirit is God's power, that is, God's aid for a particular task. In the New Testament Paul and John teach a Trinity. They, along with Mt 28:18–20, are the basis for the Christian belief in a triune God. In all of Mk, there is no clear indication that the spirit is a person. In Mk 1:10, even though the words *as a dove* may indicate some corporeal form, this does not necessarily indicate that the spirit is a person, nor need the phrase mean anything more than a visible appearance of God's aid — if it means that much, cf. *d*) below. For the following reasons we think that Mark is teaching that God's power descended to the Nazarene: (1) the passage conforms to the Old Testament usage of "the spirit"; (2) there is no clear indication that Mark ever teaches that the spirit is a person; (3) the Synoptic tradition in general is more primitive than Paul's and John's and, except for Mt 28:18–20, does not deal explicitly and clearly with the Trinity; (4) finally, the possibility of substantial revelation until the death of the last apostle allows for development of New Testament teaching on the identity of the Spirit.

c) *The spirit descended upon him.* The translation we prefer to the *upon* of Kleist (*eis* of the Greek text) is *to*. The Greek word usually means *into*. But English prepositions are used so elastically that *to* seems best. *To* fits better with the verb *saw*. Whatever translation is preferred, 1:12 shows that, whether *to* or *upon* or *into*, God's spirit was with Jesus: "Without delay, the spirit impelled him to go out into the desert" (1:12).

d) *God's power descended as a dove.* Note well that Mark is speaking in a simile, *as*. God's power is not a dove, but like a dove. The most evident meaning seemingly would be that a bodily form was seen by Jesus. But why as a *dove*? Any explanation is problematical. There is some evidence of rabbinic usage, contemporaneous to the New Testament, in which the dove is used in reference to Gen 1:2. Therefore Mark may be indicating that the figure of the dove is a symbol of Jesus' being the new creation. If this is so, Mark is teaching that God has begun a new supercreation.

We may summarize what the spirit's descending to him as a dove means. Jesus had God's power for some mission. The symbol of the dove may teach that the effect of the spirit may be a Markan expression of the Pauline new creature (cf. 2 Cor 5:17), which Jesus began and the whole Christ is.

e) In 1:10, then, Mark teaches that during a divine manifestation Jesus received God's power for a special task.

3. In 1:11 Mark teaches that God's witness is that the Nazarene is his unique Son. His mission is to be God's messianic servant.

a) *A voice rang out upon the air.* Literally this means *a voice from the heavens.* The literal translation is important since *from the heavens* continues the theophany of 1:10 and is one of the three biblically special occurrences of these two verses. God is still bearing witness.

b) What is the voice? We find the expression "daughter of a voice" (*bath qol*) in rabbinic literature. Although this expression had many meanings among the Jews, by referring to it Mark at the very least teaches that God himself stands behind the message given.

c) What was said was: "You are my beloved son: with you I am well pleased." Mark has echoes of several Old Testament passages in this phrase, especially Ps 2:7 ("You are my son; this day I have begotten you") and Is 42:1 ("Here is my servant, whom I behold, my chosen one with whom I am pleased"). There is little difference in biblical usage between "beloved" and "unique." Somehow Jesus is God's unique Son. Too, because of Mark's allusion to Is 42, Jesus is the servant of Yahweh. As a servant of Yahweh, Jesus summarizes in himself the elect of God, the people of Israel. Mark's combination of the beloved Son by excellence and the servant of Yahweh, Israel, is striking. Jesus is the expected redeemer whom we call the Messiah. But he is more than this; he is also God's unique Son.

Mark does not explain how Jesus is God's messianic servant. We know it is by reason of the hypostatic union, but it took three centuries to crystalize this terminology. Suffice it to say that the basis for evolution in Christological theology is found in Mark's singular combination of the "beloved son-servant."

Perhaps, too, Mark has given a basis for further Christological development. For the Nazarene is being *told* that he is God's Son and God's servant.

Did he know this before? This question is altogether distinct from asking *when* Jesus became God's Son. He was God's Son at the moment of the incarnation. The query also differs from asking when Jesus either had divine knowledge or was divinely conscious of being God's Son. This, too, was the moment of the incarnation.

The question refers to his human consciousness, i.e., a previous, unformed, subjective, and human experience of being God's Son and Messiah. More fully, the query is this: Did Jesus not grow in a humanly deeper realization of being God's Son and Messiah? Did he not realize at this time by God's word and spirit, in his human consciousness, that he was God's Son and Messiah? Did he not increase in this conscious realization (as every child grows into conscious realization and responsibility of adulthood) from Nazareth through Galilee to Calvary? Progress in depth psychology may permit theology to make Jesus as human as Mark presents him, while leaving him divine.

In other words, may we not assert that Jesus saw God's power and heard God's attestation of his messiahship and divine sonship and realized more fully than he had for the first thirty years of his life that he was indeed God, was God's Messiah? We believe Mark is giving a basis for saying this and that this simply means that "The Word really became man." It is less than saying "Jesus became angry" (3:6) or "Jesus snorted like a horse" (1:43, cf. Greek). Mark's Jesus is as human as you and I, human enough to be tempted by the devil (1:12 f.).

But do not be trapped into taking for granted that this passage is statistical, that is, a factual report of what actually took place on the banks of the Jordan. If we were to make an investigation of the psychology of Jesus based on 1:9–11, we would be presuming that these verses are factual, and we are not certain of that. In Mk 14:32–42, we will return to this intriguing search into the human psychology of Jesus.

d) Of importance in 1:9–11 is Mark's inspired teaching. This teaching is that time and eternity become one in a divine man. God witnessed that *The Man* was his unique Son, his messianic servant. Strange it is that *The Man's* first act under the impulse of God's spirit was to be tempted by the devil (1:12 f.)!

Relating 1:9–11 to the entire Gospel of Mark. Jesus is God's unique Son. He has God's spirit. Throughout the rest of the Gospel Mark will detail what it means to be God's beloved. He will apply it also for Christians, God's other beloved sons.

CONDEMNATION OR LIFE (Mk 3:1-6)

¹Once again, he went into the synagogue. A man with one arm withered was present. ²Now Jesus was being narrowly watched, to see whether he would heal him on the Sabbath. The purpose was to bring a charge against him. ³"Rise, and come forward," he said to the man with the withered arm. ⁴He then said to them: "Is it right on the Sabbath to do an act of kindness, or must one inflict evil? to save a life, or must one kill?" But they remained silent. ⁵Then, glancing round at them in anger, and deeply grieved at the hardness of their hearts, he said to the man: "Stretch out your arm." ⁶He stretched it out, and his arm was fully restored. The Pharisees walked out at once and consulted with the Herodians to plot against his life.

General context. From 1:14 to 8:26, we are in the second general part of Mark's Gospel: Jesus preaches the good news of God's kingdom, and the various responses to this preaching.

We have chosen 3:1-6 to underline Mark's teaching about the human failure of Jesus, to whom the persecuted and misunderstood Romans for whom he was writing his Gospel were to be loyal. These six verses fall within the particular unity formed by 2:1-3:6. This section of Mark's Gospel pictures a crescendo of opposition to Jesus. It goes from silent criticism (2:8) through the Scribes' questioning Jesus' disciples (2:16) to Jesus' being directly challenged (2:18 and 2:24). Finally, in 3:6, we read about the plot to put Jesus to death.

In the midst of this crescendo of conflicts, Mark teaches in 2:1-12 that the Man brings God's word, God's healing, and God's praise. Mark also gives Jesus' teachings on the forgiveness of sins (2:1-17), on fasting, on the new type of membership in the new covenant (2:18-22), and on the Sabbath (2:23-3:6).

Literary form of 3:1-6. Mark subordinates a miracle to a pronouncement story: "Is it right on the Sabbath to do an act of kindness or must one inflict evil? to save a life or must one kill?"

In sum, Mark teaches in 3:1-6 that the misunderstood Jesus brings condemnation or life.

Exegesis of 3:1-6.

1. (3:1 f.) *Once again, he went into the synagogue. A man*

with one arm withered was present. *Now Jesus was being narrowly watched, to see whether he would heal him on the Sabbath. The purpose was to bring a charge against him.*

There is no special problem of interpretation. A paraphrase of the text would go as follows: A cripple was in the synagogue when Jesus entered. Spies, unidentified until 3:6, were in the synagogue on the Sabbath. They were watching to see if Jesus would cure on the Sabbath.

2. Concerning the Sabbath, the Pharisees and Jesus differed radically. As a group, the Pharisees taught that the Sabbath law could be broken only if a man's life were somehow endangered. Jesus' attitude was that the Sabbath "was made for man" (Mk 2:27). As a result, any ordinary inconvenience, according to Jesus' interpretation, would set the Sabbath obligation aside. This split concerning the Sabbath can hardly be exaggerated. In most of his ethical teaching, Jesus differed only slightly from the Jewish religious leaders of his day, but here there was radical divergence.

It is true that he appealed to no other human authorities as they usually did. He condemned evil Pharisees (cf. Mt 23), but so did other Jewish leaders, including sincere Pharisees. They, too, would agree with his teachings on charity, justice, sincerity, the purity of the temple.

His teaching on the Sabbath, therefore, is the all-important difference. After all, they would say, was not the Sabbath's keeping a divine law? Were it not for the carpenter's attitude toward the Sabbath, good and pious Jews could have accepted him as another teacher. But the Sabbath, so they would have reasoned, was made not for man, but for God!

3. (3:3 f.) *"Rise, and come forward,"* he said to the man with the withered arm. He then said to them: "Is it right on the Sabbath to do an act of kindness, or must one inflict evil? to save a life, or must one kill?" But they remained silent.

With the command, *"Rise, and come forward,"* Jesus accepted the unstated challenge. His query is not a general principle and should not be understood as such. No sincere Pharisee would deny that, Sabbath or no Sabbath, one should not inflict evil or

kill. And it was precisely there that these Pharisees were caught.
For they, the "holy" ones of Israel according to their own thinking, were ambushing Jesus. They were looking for an excuse to
trap him. They remained silent, lest he make the comparison
more explicit. He could have pointed the general comparison
between right and wrong to the particular application of his healing and their ambushing and plotting death (cf. 3:6). Silence is
the only safety for the caught spy and bushwacker.

4. (3:5 f.) *Then, glancing around at them in anger, and deeply
grieved at the hardness of their hearts, he said to the man: "Stretch
out your arm." He stretched it out, and his arm was fully restored.
The Pharisees walked out at once and consulted with the Herodians to plot against his life.*

Jesus' word effortlessly effected the lifegiving miracle. He became angry and mourned the deliberate obduracy of his enemies.
The religious and civil leaders condemned themselves by plotting
his death.

a) *Then, glancing around at them in anger and deeply grieved
at the hardness of their hearts.* With these words, Mark delineates
a very human struggle between a good man who is purposely mis-
judged and a "just" group of religious rulers who refuse to accept
God's evident work. Mt 12:12 and Lk 14:10 omit the anger.
Surely the anger of Jesus was just, for he was sinless — but it
was anger, a very human emotion, nonetheless.

b) *Hardness of heart* is best understood as an intentional act
of refusing evidence, rather than an emotional feeling. The sin was
willed. The evidence of goodness was in front of these evil men
and they rejected it.

c) The healing is performed effortlessly. Jesus had done nothing but speak. The strictest interpretation of the Sabbath law
did not forbid talking. But the conclusion was, *The Pharisees
walked out at once and consulted with the Herodians to plot
against his life.*

d) The "Herodians" is a difficulty. There was no sect of Herodians comparable to Pharisees and Essenes. Nor was there a
Herodian party similar to the American Democrat or Republican

parties. The word most likely refers to some men who favored or were friends of Herod Antipas. Also the Pharisees and Herod generally had little time for each other and as a consequence another difficulty arises in their leaguing together. Considerations of this kind take for granted the historicity of Mark's note on the Herodians and Pharisees, and as noted previously, we are not concerned with that in this commentary. But, for the sake of argument if we grant the historicity, sin makes strange bedfellows. And with this in mind, the problem is minor.

Relating 3:1–6 to the entire Gospel of Mark. It is obvious that it is too early in the historical career of Jesus to consider the mention of a death plot as a chronological detail. Mark is not trying to put 2:1–3:6 into a period which would have occurred a few weeks or months after Jesus' public career had begun. Mark is adding to his picture of the human and failing Jesus of Nazareth.

We have seen Jesus as learning that he was God's Son and the servant of Yahweh (1:9–11). Jesus had experienced his mastery over men, his prophetlike teaching, and the power over devils and sickness (1:2–45). In 2:1–3:6, he emerges as the lover and healer of sinners and the sick. As the man, he has authority over God's institution, the Sabbath. But he also feels at home with sinners, brings joy as does a bridegroom, and becomes angry.

Most important in 2:1–3:6 for Mark, the "just," i.e., the Scribes and Pharisees, are responding to this enigmatic character. To what purpose for Mark are Jesus' masterful power over sickness and devils and authority to teach, when his death is plotted by the greatest power of Israel? The man is failing to convert the ones to whom he has been sent as God's Son and servant.

The division in 3:1–6 is sharply cut. Jesus in anger and tears is opposed to the insincere Pharisees' plot to murder. His human failure has begun. The shadow of Calvary's cross dawned early for Mark. In encountering Jesus, man chooses condemnation or life.

A THEOPHANY OF JESUS, WHO CAN SAVE
FROM DEATH (Mk 6:45–52)

⁴⁵Without delay he obliged his disciples to re-enter the boat
and go in advance to a place on the other shore opposite Beth-
saida, while he himself would dismiss the crowd. ⁴⁶After bidding
the people farewell, he withdrew to the mountains to pray.

⁴⁷Night had fallen and the boat was far out at sea, while he
was still on land; ⁴⁸but when he saw them in distress, trying to
make headway — for the wind was against them — he came toward
them during the last part of the night, walking upon the sea,
and would have passed them by. ⁴⁹But seeing him walk upon
the sea, they thought it was a ghost and cried aloud. ⁵⁰They all
had seen him and were perplexed. He at once, however, addressed
them, and said to them: "Take courage! It is I! Do not be afraid!"

⁵¹He then climbed up to join them in the boat. The wind
subsided; and they were utterly beside themselves. ⁵²The truth is,
they had not yet learned the lesson at the multiplication of the
loaves; on the contrary, their minds were a perfect blank.

General context. In this sixth and final section of his second
part, Mark presents Jesus' ministry beyond Galilee. To summarize
Mark's teaching in this lengthy division, extending from 6:14 to
8:26, ask the following, "What response should be given to Jesus,
whoever he is?"

Mark first gives stories to raise the question of who Jesus is
without answering it (6:14–29). Through the rest of these chapters, Mark gives various responses to Jesus to encourage loyalty.
Active faith, not amazement, even in the Eucharist (6:30–44;
8:1–26) should be paid to a man who can walk on waters (6:45–
52), feed multitudes (6:30–44; 8:1–9), give sight to the blind
(8:22–26) and hearing to the deaf (6:53–56; 7:31–37).

For Mark, one may always ask, "Who is Jesus?" A compre-
hensive response is never possible. An active living is Mark's existential approach to Jesus. Thus, Mark gives a list of sins (7:1–23)
which prevent active loyalty. He also invites the Gentile Romans
to become as needy as children in order to ask Jesus for crumbs.
They will receive life in return (7:24–30).

We have chosen 6:45–52 to show what Mark means by responding to Jesus. As we shall see, the Romans are thus taught to
be active participators in Christian life, not mere spectators.

Literary form of 6:45–52: a miracle story. A miracle story is a literary form which the early Church used to encourage converts to accept Jesus. Elements of the miracle story are: (1) the circumstances of an illness or difficulty; (2) the wonder worked by Jesus; (3) the effect on the crowd. For other examples of miracle stories in Mk, cf. 1:25–28; 1:29–31; 4:35–40.

Summary of Mark's teachings in 6:45–52. Moved by compassion for his struggling friends, Jesus walks on the sea to them, only to consent to pass by when he sees their fright at his phantomlike figure. His intention is changed to a word of comfort to answer their cry. He gets into the boat and the wind falls. The obtuse disciples, so familiar with him, the human, are again amazed at his power and compassion.

Exegesis of 6:45–52.

1. (6:45–48b) The compassion of Jesus makes him walk to his friends.

a) In 6:45 f., Mark sets the scene with special emphasis on Jesus. It is Jesus who makes his disciples leave. He himself dismisses the crowd. Finally, the Man goes to pray.

b) The better division seems to be 6:47–48b. The sentence should run: *Night had fallen and the boat was far out at sea, while he was still on land; but when he saw them in distress, trying to make headway — for the wind was against them — he came toward them, during the last part of the night, walking upon the sea* . . . .

Mark mentions twice that it was late. Jesus was separated from the boat by a goodly distance. The disciples were rowing against a contrary wind which, however, was not a tempest. Jesus came, walking on the sea.

Someone knowledgeable in the Old Testament who read that Jesus walked on water would understand that Mark is teaching at least that Jesus had divine attributes. He would identify Jesus with the divine attribute of wisdom — or understand him to be divine as such. An Old Testament student would have concluded this, first of all, from the general Old Testament teaching that God controlled the water: one who walked on water controlled it and

consequently at least shared in the divine power. Second, he would
have seen the event in the light of Sir 24:5: "Through the deep
abyss, I wandered." The word for "abyss" in the Greek translation
of the Old Testament called the Septuagint is *bathei abusson*.
Although the Hebrew part of this verse has not yet been found,
it is probably *tehom*. This alludes to Gen 1:2, which taught that
the divinity ruled over the abyss. Moreover, from Ps 17(18):15–17;
Ps 68(69): 2 f.; 2 Sam 22:5, the Old Testament student would have
understood that someone who could walk on water had power over
the nether world, over Sheol, over death. With this simple allusion to walking on water, Mark teaches anyone who had even
the simplest introduction to Old Testament figures that Jesus has
divine attributes and is lord of death.

2. (6:48c–50a) *And he would have passed them by. But seeing
him walk upon the sea, they thought it was a ghost and cried
out aloud. They all had seen and were perplexed.*

In summary, Mark teaches the following. Seeing their fright, he
consents to turn aside. But they, being frightened by the phantomlike apparition, cry out.

He would have passed them by. This expression is troublesome.
Why did Jesus come out to them? It could hardly have been only
to pass by. Why, then, did he tend to pass by? The Greek word
ēthelen can mean, "to be willing, of consent rather than desire."
In this phrase, Mark gives no cause for this consent. The fact is
that Jesus, after coming out to his disciples, consented to pass
them by. Too, in 6:51, Jesus did get into the boat. Thus we are
confronted by a paradox: either Jesus walked on the water to no
purpose or he showed fickleness. As we shall see, the solution is
that Mark is not giving a statistic, a factual report, but a teaching.
And his teaching is that fright prevents Jesus, but a cry draws
him. To understand this, we must look closely at the words of the
text and understand precisely what Mark means by awe and fear.

The facts of the text are these: (1) Jesus began to consent to
go by, even though he had come out to them. (2) He changed
his mind and entered the boat. (3) The disciples were perplexed
at the ghost. (4) The disciples feared, lacked courage, and had

misunderstood the multiplication of the loaves.

The resolution of the difficulties presented by these facts is in the Markan technical meaning for "awe" (here, *perplexity*) and "fear."

Thesis: For Mark, both fear and awe are qualities of spectators, whether Christian or non-Christian. Both fear and awe are poor qualities. Faith, that is, participation or involvement, is a Markan ideal of piety and includes the notion of understanding in act.

Proofs: (a) In Mark's Gospel, the people who are in amazement or in fear either are Christians who are lacking something, or are enemies to Christ. Those in the synagogue are amazed (1:21, 23, 29; 6:2); so too are Christianity's persecutors (13:9) or disbelievers (6:6). The crowd is in awe (11:18; 12:37); but Mark designates the crowd as those outside (4:1–11). The crowd is taught in "parables" so that they will not understand (4:12; 7:14, 18). The crowd presses Jesus (3:9; 5:24, 31) and keeps him from those he wishes to aid (2:4; 5:31). Also in amazement, after fearing (12:12), are Jesus' enemies (12:17). Herod feared John, but killed him (6:20–29). Pilate was in amazement at Jesus, but ordered him killed (15:5, 44). The woman with the hemorrhage shrank from fear and rose only when told of her belief (5:33, 36).

b) The clearest definition Mark gives of fear and awe is in describing Jesus' disciples. In 4:40 f., in the context of the story of the storm on the sea, the disciples are in awe and fear; when, lacking faith, they ask who Jesus is: "He also said to them, 'Why are you so timid?' and, 'How is it that you are still without faith?' For they had been struck with great fear, and had said to one another, 'Who really is this man? Why, even wind and sea obey him!' " In other words, fear and awe prevent faith and keep a man from realizing who Jesus is.

c) One may object to the interpretation of awe and fear as qualities of spectators since Mark also predicates these qualities of Jesus. In 6:5 f. Jesus is amazed. In 14:33, Jesus shudders in terror. But in these two places, Jesus himself is a spectator. "He could not work any miracle there. . . . Wondering at their unbelief, he went on a teaching journey through the villages round

about" (6:5 ff.). And, in Gethsemani, he feared to do God's will
(as we shall see below). Mark is saying no more than what Heb
5:8 says: "Son though he was, he learned obedience through what
he suffered, and after he had been raised to the heights of perfection, he became to all who obey him the cause of eternal salvation" (5:8–10). Jesus — humanly speaking — grew in holiness.
The act of love on the cross was his most perfect choosing of God's
will. It was more perfect than the (sinless) spectatorship of
Gethsemani, so Mark would have put it. Before the Nazarenes
and in Gethsemani, Mark tells us, the Nazarene was a spectator,
not a participant.

To return then to our facts, Jesus came to them but would have
passed by. Why? Because they feared and misunderstood (6:52).
Why did he then enter the boat? Because they cried out, an
initial and imperfect beginning of participation. As the disciples
had done before, so the Christians in Mark's time made Jesus a
phantom. Thus Mark advised the Christians in Rome to accept
Jesus as he is — praying and yet walking on waters — not as you
make him to be. A greater appeal for realism and participation in
early Church Christianity would be hard to find.

3. (6:50b–51b) *He at once, however, addressed them, and
said to them: "Take courage! It is I! Do not be afraid!" He then
climbed up to join them in the boat.* Jesus changes his intention to
reassure them of his reality by telling them not to fear: "It is I!"
In Mark's theological terminology, *egō eimi* probably means no
more than "It is I." Mark is neither so profound nor so advanced
as John, who uses this phrase to mean Yahweh.

4. (6:51c f.) *The wind subsided. And they were utterly beside
themselves. The truth is, they had not yet learned the lesson at
the multiplication of the loaves; on the contrary, their minds were
a perfect blank.* By these sentences Mark teaches that the apostles
were overwhelmed by his power, and did not realize that they
must participate in Christianity.

a) In 6:51c, the wind falls. The Markan account gives no
reason to attribute this to any action of Jesus.

b) In 6:52, the reason that the disciples are amazed is their obduracy. The verb is taken from the same root as that of the "hardness of heart" we have seen in 3:5 concerning the Pharisees. What should they have understood about the loaves? They should have grasped two points. The first is that Jesus gives life. The second is that they participate in the giving: "Taking the loaves and the two fish into his hands, he looked up to heaven and, after saying grace, broke the loaves into portions, which he gave to his disciples to serve to the people." Without this food, the people would not have eaten. Without the apostles' help, the lifegiving food would not have been distributed. They had not understood his power or their own need to participate.

Relating 6:42–52 to the entire Gospel of Mark. Here Mark has continued teaching the Romans that Jesus is both human and divine. Jesus, God, was human enough to pray and to consent to pass by when misunderstood. Jesus, Man, was divine enough to walk on water and to require an active response of faith. Mark is no docetist, i.e., one who holds that Jesus *seemed* to be a man. He teaches his readers to cease being frightened at an incarnate God. Jesus can give life. Misunderstanding of his power, fright at his divine body, or amazement at his saving power must be put aside. At least, cry out. Then courage!

THE CHRISTIAN'S IDEAL: THE "GIMME" OF A CHILD (Mk 10:13–16)

¹³One day people brought little children to him, that he might lay his hands on them; but the disciples scolded them for doing so. ¹⁴Jesus saw this and became indignant. "Let the little children come to me," he said to them, "and do not stop them: to such belongs the kingdom of God. ¹⁵I assure you, whoever does not receive the kingdom of God as does a little child, will not enter it." ¹⁶He then folded them in his arms and, laying his hands on them spoke a fervent blessing.

General context. Verses 13 to 16 of Chapter 10 form the third section of Mark's third part. The third part of the Gospel in general is the preparation of the future good news: Victory through the passion, death, and resurrection (8:27–13:37). In 10:1–32, Mark gives Jesus' teachings on adultery, on how to enter the kingdom, and on wealth. In verses 1 to 12 of Chapter 10, Mark teaches that marriage is forever. The "gimme" of a child is offered as a Christian's ideal. And, following the section of our concern, in 10:17–31, Mark teaches that poverty may buy life; God alone can and will give it.

We chose 10:13–16 because it brings out Jesus' warmth toward children, one of his most human qualities. Too, the literary beauty of these verses is striking.

Literary form. The story is a pronouncement. In fact there are three unforgettable pronouncements in these few verses. (1) "Suffer the children to come to me." (2) "To such as these belongs the kingdom of God." (3) "Whoever does not receive the kingdom of God, as does a little child, will not enter it."

Summary of Mark's teachings in 10:13–16. Mark teaches that the divine kingdom is to be entered by receiving the supreme power of God who directs us to a supernatural end.

Exegesis of 10:13–16.

1. *(10:13) One day, people brought little children to him, that he might lay his hands on them: but the disciples scolded them for doing so.* In sum, this verse teaches the following. Parents or perhaps older children brought youths to be touched by Jesus. The disciples scolded their elders and stopped the children. We do not know who actually brought the children, since an impersonal construction, "they" (= *people*, in above translation) is used.

The children (*paidia*) who are brought may range in age from six to about twelve. Lk (18:15) makes them babies (*brephē*). The disciples tried to prevent their being presented to Jesus. Mark does not tell us why. Any conjecture is just that. Whatever it was, the disciples were on such familiar terms with Jesus that they thought they could take care of him (cf. 6:35 f.).

The children had been brought to be touched by Jesus. Again, Mark tells us no more. Was it so that Jesus could bless them, as Isaac had blessed the children of Joseph who had been brought to him? (Cf. Gen 48:14.)

2. (10:14) *Jesus saw this and became indignant. "Let the little children come to me,"* he said to them, *"and do not stop them; to such as these belongs the kingdom of God."*

Jesus, indignant, wanted them to come to life. Mark teaches Jesus' human love for children. He also teaches that they may be baptized. These have the *sine qua non* to receive God's power.

a) The word "indignant" (*ēganaktēsen*) is very strong. It is used of Jesus only here in the entire New Testament. Once again, Mark shows the humanity of the man who became very vexed at his own disciples when they tried to prevent children's coming to him.

b) *Do not stop them* (*mē kōluete*) is more than a mere permission to approach Jesus. It is a technical term in the early Church, like our *imprimatur*, against anyone who would hinder someone from baptism, that is, from following Christ. The great Protestant theologian Oscar Cullmann argues convincingly that *kōlein* (to stop) is a technical term for baptism with water (cf. also Acts 8:36; 10:47; Mt 3:13 f.; parallels to Mk 10:13–16). In context, then, this is Mark's and the early Church's answer to those who forbid baptism to children *paidia* i.e., more than six years of age. Luke has extended the age limit to *brephē*, that is, to babies, in 18:15 of his Gospel.

c) The kingdom of God or of heaven is a term of complex meaning and we refer our readers to the dictionaries and reference works mentioned in the bibliography for more complete discussions. In brief, the kingdom is basically God's reign for God's supernatural end. The biblical notion of God's kingdom is a dynamic concept. At the time of Mark's Gospel the kingdom was present in Christ's preaching, man's dispositions, and in the Church. It was past in Israel's existence, which prepared for Christ. It will be future in the Parousia, or final, eschatological coming of Christ. All of these times, these states, and these qualities are found in the concept of "God's kingdom."

Akin to the "Day of the Lord," the kingdom of God stresses God's reign while the Day stresses time. The kingdom is the result of God's power or spirit. To attempt a more precise description

than the one given above: the kingdom of God is God's earthly
and dynamic reign bringing about the perfection of Christ.

d) *To such as these belongs the kingdom of heaven* is used
elsewhere in the New Testament only in the beatitudes of Mt
5:3–10. As we shall see, Mark agrees with Matthew. Mark expresses
the Matthean "poor," i.e., the lacking or needy, by the concept
of a child.

3. One of Jesus' pronouncements appears in 10:15: *Whoever
does not receive the kingdom of God as does a little child, will
not enter it.* The sentence is vital for Christianity. All can enter
life only if they will welcome it as a child welcomes a gift. The
word *receive* (*deksētai*) means to welcome one as a guest, with
all the connotations of the generous and open-hearted Semitic
hospitality.

What is the quality that makes children fit for the kingdom?
In rabbinic teaching the child was almost despicable. In Roman
law a child was without rights. Neither by nature nor in the
Jewish thinking of the time was a child truly either simple, humble, docile, "innocent," or "pure." Only maturity could win these
virtues. For Jesus, on the other hand, the child's insufficiency and
asking-ability, his "gimme," made him qualify for the kingdom.
Jesus saw the lack in a child as a good example of the *anawim*, the
"poor," the "needy" person of the Old Testament. Mark's
"gimme" — even to a child filling his mouth, stuffing his pockets,
and loading his hands with candy — is the *sine qua non* of an
ideal Christian. A child knows how to welcome (*deksētai*) with
hands outstretched to be filled with God's gift of his kingdom.

4. In 10:16, Jesus lovingly embraced the children, touched and
blessed them. They had come merely to be touched. But he
*folded them in his arms, and laying his hand on them spoke a
fervent blessing.* He gave more than he had been asked.

Relating 10:13–16 to the entire Gospel of Mark. Mark himself,
probably well-to-do, had known the veneer of sophistication. In
these verses, he taught that only the pomposity of pretense hin-
ders a man from God. Kings, princes, and the contented non-
chalant could ossify in their self-sufficiency. The man who could

say "gimme" to the indignant Nazarene, Son of God, would run into life by washing away dirt through the waters of baptism. Only a child can run after a gift. He knows that he has no reason for being given the gift. In fact, he doesn't think of himself. But the child wants the gift with all the sparkle of insufficiency. Awe ceases with the child's plunge into the life which is the Man!

THE DEATHFUL SORROWS OF THE SOLITARY SON OF MAN — DESERTED BY HIS OWN, IN SHUDDERING HORROR BEFORE GOD'S WILL (Mk 14:32-42)

[32]They now came to a place called Gethsemani. "Rest here," he said to his disciples, "till I finish praying." [33]Then, taking Peter, James, and John with him, he gave way to terror and weariness, [34]and said to them: "I am plunged in sorrow, enough to break my heart! Stay here and keep awake." [35]He then went a short distance forward, threw himself on the ground, and prayed that, if it were possible, he might be spared the ordeal. [36]He said: "Abba, Father, you can do all things! Spare me this cup! No, not what I will, but what you will!"

[37]He then came back and found them sleeping. "Simon," he said to Peter, "are you sleeping? Were you not able to stay awake one hour? [38]Keep awake and pray, all of you, that you may not succumb to temptation. The spirit is willing, but the flesh is weak." [39]Again he went away and prayed, using the same words. [40]On returning, he again found them sleeping. Their eyes had been yielding to drowsiness; and they were at a loss what to say to him. [41]When he returned the third time, he said to them: "So you continue to sleep and rest! It is enough. The hour has struck. Look, the Son of Man is being betrayed into the hands of sinful men! [42]Rise; let us go. Look, my betrayer is close at hand."

General context. We are here in the fourth general part of Mark's Gospel, the act of victory which includes 14:1 to 16:8. Chapter 14 may be summarized as a narrative of events which culminate in the arrest. Therein we find the plot to kill Jesus, the betrayal, the preparation for the Pasch, and Jesus' foretelling that one of the twelve would betray him. Mark has also told of the institution of the covenantal eucharistic sacrifice. Finally, Mark gives a group of sayings on the scandal of the disciples, the resurrection, and Peter's denial. Jesus then leaves the Cenacle and goes to Gethsemani.

We have chosen 14:32–42 because Jesus' humanity is Mark's special contribution to the Gospel mosaic of Jesus, and that humanity is forcefully limned in these verses. The description of the fearful, lonely man who shudders before God's will is the Markan reason for life. Such a description is found in the Bible uniquely in this pericope.

Literary form. One of the events in the passion narrative, 14:32–42, is for the most part statistical, i.e., historical.

Summary of Mark's teaching in 14:32–42: Jesus takes three of the disciples apart from the rest. Then, alone and in anguish, he three times prays to his Father to remove his sufferings. The three disciples meanwhile sleep. As Jesus finishes, Judas comes.

Exegesis of 14:32–42.

1. (14:32) *They now come to a place called Gethsemani. "Rest here," he said to his disciples, "till I finish praying."* Entering the lower slope of the Mount of Olives, Jesus tells the disciples to wait while he raises his heart and mind to God.

2. (14:33) *Then, taking Peter, James, and John with him, he gave way to terror and weariness.* With three of his followers, Jesus starts having an amazed terror and anguish.

We do not know why the three were brought. Later, in 14:34 and 38, they are told to watch and pray.

"Terror" and "weariness" translate two Greek terms which refer to an intense emotional state. The first, *ekthambeisthai,* means literally "to be alarmed," "to be distressed." It is part of the Markan vocabulary for awe (cf. p. 21 ff.) which left the Man momentarily as a spectator in Christianity. The second, *adēmonein,* means "to be in anxiety, distressed, troubled." Modern scholars such as Vincent Taylor and Ernst Lohmeyer have shown that these Greek terms describe the utmost degree of unbounded horror and suffering. Matthew softened the phrase to "Jesus gave way to sorrow" (26:37). Luke omitted it completely (22:39–46). Luke has added to the description that Jesus' anguish was so terrifying that his sweat became clots of blood (22:44).

This prayer is the only example (and the Our Father is no exception) which we have of the contents of the prayer of Jesus of Nazareth. At once consoling and frightening, the prayer leaves us wondering at the cause of such an almost deranged state.

Avoiding both the macabre imaginative and the pietistic unrealistic, we think that Mark has described one of the most strikingly human states any man has gone through. Before, when discussing 1:9–11, we stepped gingerly, attempting to avoid making Jesus less than man. Here, too, we must avoid the same. Later, in our concluding remarks on 14:32–42, we shall return to this subject.

3. (14:34a) Whatever the cause, Jesus' overwhelming grief is enough to cause death. Kleist has caught the feeling in his translation, *I am plunged in sorrow, enough to break my heart.* Heartbreak can cause death. The Greek literally means, "my soul is deeply grieved unto death," and should not be watered down. Was a miracle needed to keep this human alive to face Calvary? Would death now not have been a consolation?

4. (14:34b) "Stay here and keep awake." Ashamed or needing to be alone, Jesus leaves the three, telling them to remain and to watch. They were to look on (prayerfully?) as he becomes prostrate before God. There was to be mankind's unique experience of the incarnate God's prayer.

5. (14:35 f.) *He then went a short distance forward, threw himself on the ground, and prayed that, if it were possible he might be spared the ordeal. He said: "Abba, Father, you can do all things! Spare me this cup! No, not what I will, but what you will!"*

In sum, Mark gives an indirect and direct discourse telling how Jesus, prostrate, prayed to his Father in all confidence that the eschatological messianic time of accepting the vicarious suffering for sin might be removed, if God willed.

a) He fell to the earth. Then Mark tells the prayer twice. The two key words for understanding its contents are *hōra* (literally "hour"; Kleist: "ordeal"), and *potērion* ("cup").

b) The *hōra* in many places of the Synoptic Gospels and Jn

has the meaning of the time of fulfilling the Old Testament expectations, thus the eschatological and messianic times. It frequently connotes the period of Jesus' suffering. In Jn, the resurrection is also connoted. In 14:41, Mark gives a clear description of the word, "The hour has struck. Look, the Son of Man is being betrayed into the hands of sinful men!"

c) *Potērion*, in the Old Testament in a context of something undesired, such as we have here, is a cup of sorrow. Usually, the cup includes a punishment for sin, divine retribution. For example, Ps 74(75):9: "For a cup is in the Lord's hand, full of spiced and foaming wine; and he pours out from it. Even to the dregs they shall drain it; all the wicked of the earth shall drink." Cf. also Is 2:17–22; Jer 25:15; Ezek 23:31–34. Mark has used the cup similarly in 10:38. There is no reason to deny all of the meanings here. Jesus prayed to be delivered from the sorrows due to sin. Paul had written in a similar vein: "He was made sin for us" (2 Cor 5:21).

d) *Abba* is the Aramaic equivalent for our "Daddy," a child's familiar name for his father. The consistent use in the New Testament of the expression with its Greek equivalent may indicate a later and liturgical usage.

e) *You can do all things* needs no explanation. In Mark, Jesus clearly prays that the "what" of God's will be done! Matthew has softened the expression from Mark's "Not *what* I will" to "Not *as* I will" (Mt 26:39).

6. (14:37 f.) The disciples sleep. Jesus asks Simon if he has not the strength to keep vigil one hour. It is needed so that the solicitations to evil will not overwhelm them. Man, as dependent on God, is willing (spirit: *pneuma*); but his frail, weak nature (flesh: *sarx*) is limited.

7. (14:39) Jesus goes away to pray as before.

8. (14:40) The three, again asleep, cannot excuse themselves.

9. (14:41 f.) *When he returned the third time, he said to them: "So you continue to sleep and rest! It is enough. The hour has struck. Look, the Son of Man is being betrayed into the hands of sinful men! Rise; let us go. Look, my betrayer is close at hand."*

In summary, Mark teaches the following in these two verses. When Jesus returned the third time, he expressed his resigned melancholy at the state in which the disciples could continue, but not he. The end had come; the Man would be handed over to sinners, since the betrayer was come.

a) The forty-first verse presents some textual and translation problems. Kleist's "So you continue to sleep and rest! It is enough," could be read, "Continue to sleep and rest? It is enough." Too, the "It is enough" meaning for *apeksei* is almost unknown in the *koinē*, the Greek spoken by the man of the street of New Testament times and used in Mark's Gospel. Whatever is to be said of these problems, the words certainly signify a state of resigned melancholy on the part of Jesus because the three continued in sleep after being warned of impending evil and after seeing his own shock and dread.

b) The term "Son of Man" is one of Mark's favorites for Jesus, as we saw in the special introduction to his Gospel, p. 6. The judgment, "sinners," echoes harshly on the curing physician and the man who ate and drank with sinners!

c) Excursus on the contents of Jesus' prayer in Gethsemani: From what did Jesus beg to be removed? What precisely was the hour and the cup? Why did the agony cause the amazed terror described by Mark and the clots of blood of Luke?

Uniting the facts in Mark's Gospels, explained above, we know: (1) Jesus was in a profound emotional state (14:33); (2) The hour and cup may be summarized as meaning the eschatological and messianic time of accepting vicarious suffering for sin: in 14:41 f., Mark at least partially explains the hour as meaning the betrayal of the Son of Man into the hands of sinners. (3) Jesus prayed in 14:36 that God's will, not his, be done.

To reach an understanding of Jesus' prayer, we ought to keep in mind the following points:

1) Mark's passion account is, in general, historical.

2) Jesus was always *divinely* conscious, i.e., he had a previous and subjective experience that his "I" was that of the Second Person of the Trinity.

3) We just do not know how much Jesus as Man understood of what lay before him. His human knowledge may not have grasped the meaning of the trial and suffering he was to undergo. The scholastic idea that Jesus possessed the beatific vision, infused knowledge, and acquired knowledge is presently under study by theologians. It is not the place of this book to decide the question of Jesus' human knowledge. It is, moreover, as we have seen, not to the point to decide. Mark is speaking of an experience, a felt realization which every scholastic permits in Jesus' acquired knowledge. But Jesus' knowledge is so interrelated to the experience Mark describes that numbers 4 to 7 below must be mentioned.

4) Ignorance does not make Jesus less perfectly human. The New Testament and theology require that he be perfectly human, i.e., as normally a man as any man — sin excluded. The New Testament does not teach that he was a *perfect human*, but only *perfectly human!* The New Testament authors describe the Man they had talked to, eaten with, laughed with, or heard about from others — not an abstract imagined human. He is not less perfectly human, for example, if we assert that Joseph taught him how to be a carpenter than if we assert that he knew more about carpentry work than the world's most skilled worker in wood.

5) We think, therefore, that Jesus acquired knowledge of his own fate from prayerful study of Is 53 and a deep insight into tion of the Old Testament called the Septuagint is abusson. his enemies. We think the degree to which the prophecies about his crucifixion and resurrection found in the Gospels are a later clarification of the early Church is an open question. Jesus may have known and have said no more than, "If you destroy this sanctuary I will build it up again in three days" (Jn 2:14), which need express no more than a suspicion of his murder and a trust in God. Both themes are common in the psalms.

6) Consequently, even in the agony, he could have shuddered at the *what*, as Mk 14:36 says, (not *as*) God willed. In other words, he trembled at the contents of God's will for him: his death.

7) No human intellect can penetrate the mystery of God's use of suffering to perfect man. Efficacious grace does not require suffering! Too, the mystery of suffering as beneficial for others is precisely a mystery. Jesus' human knowledge, even in the beatific vision, could not comprehend either of these. His death in the vigor of his youth may have seemed to his human knowledge a failure, a wasted life, both for himself and especially for God.

8) Jesus was humanly conscious of the fact and knew by reflection that he was sinless.

9) Jesus' will was made more perfect by suffering. "Son though he was, he learned obedience through what he suffered, and after he had been raised to the heights of perfection, he became to all who obey him the cause of eternal salvation." "It was fitting that he [the Father] . . .should by suffering raise to the heights of perfection the author of their salvation" (Heb 5:8 and 2:10). As a result, when he finished the agony, his act of loving God was more perfect than when he began.

To answer the questions placed above. What did he pray be removed? What was the hour and cup? Why the amazed terror? Jesus of Nazareth experienced for the first time that he would die after betrayal by sinners. He at first recoiled as a spectator from such a divine fate of failure. His act of love after the agony was more perfect than before. Mark's Jesus is this human! His Jesus is human enough even to say "My God, my God, why do you abandon me?" (Mk 15:35) when he does experience the crucifixion.

Relating 14:32–42 to the entire Gospel of Mark. Throughout Mark's Gospel, Jesus is the Person who gives meaning to life's sufferings, failure, and sins. The Man had experienced all but the sin in shuddering terror. Mark wrote his Gospel to and for the Christians at Rome. Now, the humanly failing and sinful Romans might decide if this Person would give value to their lives. Mark wrote to the Romans:

> It was necessary for the Son of Man to suffer much. . . . If anyone wants to be my follower, he must renounce himself and

shoulder his cross; then he may be a follower of mine. Why, he who would save his life shall lose it; but he who freely parts with his life for the sake of the gospel will save it in the end (8:31, 34 f.).

Would the Romans respond with loving loyalty? Would they imitate those who first encountered an empty grave, who "hurriedly left the tomb, for they were panic-stricken; and they did not say a word to anyone; they were so afraid" (16:8)?

CHAPTER TWO

Jesus in the Gospel According to Matthew

Historical background. The tradition of the early Church unanimously attributed the first Gospel to the apostle Matthew, but in speaking of this Gospel early writers referred to one written in Aramaic or "Hebrew," and the text of this original Gospel according to Matthew has been lost. The problem for modern biblical scholars is to show the relationship of the Aramaic or "Hebrew" Gospel of Matthew to the Greek Gospel, which is the inspired text received into the canon of Sacred Scripture. Closely linked to the relationship of the Aramaic Mt to the Greek is the whole problem of the sources for the Synoptic Gospels and their interrelations, a problem we met in our preface (cf. p. ix). Here we shall note some pertinent facts regarding the origin of the inspired, Greek text of Matthew (hereafter referred to simply as Mt, to show that we are referring to the canonical Gospel and not to the apostle Matthew) and some of the major conclusions reached by current biblical scholars.

The oldest source of information concerning this Gospel is Papias, the early Church writer whom we met when we were looking into the historical background of the Gospel according to Mark. Papias attributed to the apostle Matthew the composi-

tion of the discourses or "sayings" (*logia*) of Jesus in Aramaic.
The same testimony is given by Irenaeus, who says that Matthew,
who was preaching "among the Hebrews, produced in their
language a writing of the Gospel while Peter and Paul were
preaching and founding the Church in Rome." Origen and the
early Church historian Eusebius of Caesarea also claim that the
apostle Matthew wrote a Gospel in Aramaic, which they call
"Hebrew."

From these witnesses, we can conclude that there was in cir-
culation in the early Church a collection of Jesus' "sayings" or
"discourses," written in Aramaic. Papias said that "each one
translated them (that is, the "sayings" in the Aramaic Matthew)
as best he could," and this statement has led some to hold that
the canonical Mt is simply a translation and perhaps expansion
of the Aramaic Gospel. However there are serious difficulties
against the theory that Mt is a translation from the Aramaic.
One noted biblical scholar, John L. McKenzie, S.J., sums up
the matter in his *Dictionary of the Bible* in this way:

> It [Mt] does not show the signs of a translation; in particular
> it is difficult to retranslate Mt into an Aramaic original. There
> are some word plays . . . which are possible only in Greek. The
> citations from the Old Testament number 41, of which 21 are
> common to Mt-Mk-Lk; these 21 are all given according to the
> LXX (the Septuagint Greek text of the Old Testament), which
> makes an Aramaic original unlikely. . . . Finally, there is an evident
> dependence on Mark in almost all the narrative passages. It is
> therefore possible to maintain an Aramaic original of Mt only if
> one understands that the Greek Mt is a thorough and substantial
> revision of the Aramaic original and not a mere translation. . . .
> It follows that [the Apostle] Matthew is not the author of the
> Greek Mt.

About all we can say with certainty, then, is that the apostle
Matthew composed a "Gospel" in Aramaic of certain "sayings"
of Jesus, and that this Aramaic version was most likely one of
the sources for our present Mt. Most likely, the author (or
authors) of Mt also drew upon the Gospel according to Mark
and other sources. Although Irenaeus asserts that the Aramaic
Gospel was written while Peter and Paul were in Rome (that

is, ca. A.D. 60–65), most critics today hold that the Greek Gospel was written about A.D. 75, although there is considerable dispute about its date.

On one point, however, every critic agrees. Mt is the most Semitic or Jewish of the Gospels. The author's *Weltanschauung* is that of the Old Testament, and his thinking is as precise as a lawyer's. Thus he has a neat and orderly Gospel. As a Semite, he sees things concretely and in a totality, not in the Greek definition-division-explanation way of knowing. It is possible, as the scholar Krister Stendahl has noted, that the Gospel is the result of a school of a converted Rabbi. It was written for a Jewish-Christian community of a now unknown location, perhaps Palestine.

Importance of Mt. Almost half the Gospels for Sundays and holydays read in the liturgy for more than seventeen centuries have been taken from Mt. The other three Gospels fill in what it was seemingly thought was lacking in Mt. This use of Mt has had the most profound implications, as the reader will grasp after reflection, for shaping our outlook on Jesus.

Literary form of Mt. Mt's literary form in general is that of a gospel, that is, that literary form which groups pre-existing pericopes to tell the good news of salvation. His interpretation of the Old Testament is frequently, if not always midrashic. In other words, Mt sees in the events of Jesus' ministry present fulfillment of an Old Testament text, which did not literally refer to the fulfillment Mt teaches. By its very nature, the gospel-form requires other subforms, e.g., pronouncement stories, miracle stories, and the like.

OUTLINE OF MATTHEW'S GOSPEL

FIRST PART: (1:1–4:16).
I. Prehistory (1:1–2:23).
   A. Title: a book of Jesus, Messiah; the promised Davidic King, the awaited offspring of Abraham; the Savior (1:1).
   B. Jesus' genealogy proves him to be the divinely promised Messiah (1:2–17).
   C. The Old Testament about Jesus: Emmanuel, he will

be of a virgin; Gentiles will adore him at Bethlehem.
Called from Egypt, the cause of sorrows, and the offspring of David, he will save his people 1:18–25;
cf. below, 1:18–25).

II. After John's proclamation, Jesus accepts and begins his
messianic role (3:1–4:16).
  A. John proclaimed, "Divine judgment is at hand" (3:1–
  12).
  B. Jesus' messianic investiture, proclamation, acceptance,
  and beginning (3:13–4:16).

SECOND PART: (4:17–9:34).
  I. The Word of the Master (4:17–7:29).
    A. The Messiah's message in preview; his apostles; his
    words (4:17–25).
    B. The sermon (5:1–7:27; cf. 5:1–12 below).
  II. The Cures of the Master (8:1–9:34).
    A. Three miracle stories: opposition of Messiah to the
    Jews (8:1–17).
    B. Disciples can come from any class, if they do not re-
    ject Jesus (8:18–9:9).
    C. Persevering faith in Jesus, not pharisaic teaching about
    Israelitic holiness, leads to God's salvation (9:10–34).

THIRD PART: (9:35–12:50).
  I. Missionaries: rules; behavior in suffering (9:35–11:1;
  cf. below 10:24–33).
  II. Jesus' disciples, not followers of the Jewish religion, are
  doing God's will (11:2–12:50).
    A. God's will is revealed only to Jesus' followers, not to
    those who reject him (11:2–30).
    B. Mercy, not pharisaic teaching, is God's will (12:1–
    21).
    C. Jesus' disciple does God's will (12:22–50).

FOURTH PART: (13:1–16:20).
  I. "Parables" and why men should join the Church (13:1–
  52; cf. below 13:44).
  II. End of the work in Galilee (13:53–16:20).
    A. Disbelief in Nazareth; Herod's judgment; John's death
    (13:53–14:12).
    B. Salvation only in Jesus (14:13–36).
    C. A new order, not of pharisaic cultic traditions, but
    of God's law of internal morality; Peter's denseness
    (15:1–20).
    D. Gentiles, through faith, can accept the Eucharist and
    other Christian teachings. No longer Jewish teachings,
    but Peter's teaching, is God's will (15:21–16:20).

FIFTH PART: (16:21–20:34).
I. Disciples' preparation (16:21–18:35).
  A. Announcement of the destiny of Jesus and his followers (16:21–28).
  B. No longer the law and the prophets, but God's messianic Son declares God's will (17:1–8).
  C. John was Elijah; Jesus, the Messiah (17:9–13).
  D. Believers can do all things (17:14–19; no 17:20).
  E. Second announcement of the passion (17:21–23).
  F. The exempt sons pay a tax (17:23–26).
  G. The Christian family avoids scandal, tries to convert a sinner, uses mercy as its norm (18:1–35; cf. below, 18:21–35).
II. Underway (19:1–20:34).
  A. Marriage is indissoluble (19:1–9).
  B. Divinely given celibacy for God is better than marriage (19:10–12).
  C. The exemplars of the kingdom (19:13–15).
  D. Poverty brings a generous reward (19:16–20:16).
  E. To Jerusalem: those guilty of Jesus' death; his serving is the model of the highest place; the gift of faith to follow the king through suffering to victory (20:17–34).

SIXTH PART: (21:1–23:39).
I. The Master as victorious (21:1–22:46).
  A. Jesus, the promised Lord of the temple (21:1–17).
  B. A believer can imitate Jesus, even in rejecting his own people who had first refused his precursor and him (21:18–22:22).
  C. By answering essential Jewish problems, Jesus accredits himself as one able to teach about the resurrection, charity, and the Messiah (22:23–46).
II. Discourse against the Scribes and Pharisees (23:1–39).

SEVENTH PART: (24:1–28:20).
I. Victory to the persevering; punishment to the wicked; suffering for all (24:1–25:46; cf. below, 24:36–42).
II. Death and resurrection (26:1–28:20).
  A. Preparation for his death, the end of the Sinaitic covenant (26:1–16).
  B. The Passover (26:17–35).
  C. The passion narrative (26:36–27:61).
  D. The resurrection, seal of Jewish and Christian division (27:62–28:15).
  E. His final revelation: Teach God's will to all, making them the Son's (28:16–20).

The teaching of Matthew's Gospel in summary. Mark's enthusiasm and passion for the uncertain in life is lost in Mt. It is replaced by security and God's will. Both searched for and taught trust. Mark taught it in a dark plunge following after anguish. Mt taught it in the secure edifice of law brought by the king and found in the kingdom.

God's king and kingdom with its law summarize Mt's teaching. The king is the promised Davidic ruler, the fulfillment of the promises to Abraham (cf. Mt 1–2). Mt proclaims that the Emmanuel, the new Moses, has come and is with us (Mt 1:25; 28:18–20).

But God's kingdom is not joined by adhering to a human and political society, but by accepting God's revealed will. Jesus, the new Moses, the lawgiver, had the right to reveal God's will. Only he, the Son, knew it (Mt 11:25–27). He could disclose God's will because he had God's authority: "The Son of Man has authority over the Sabbath" (12:18). Finally, Jesus could manifest God's will because he showed the sign and mercy promised by Isaiah (12:15–21) and because salvation is only in him (14:13–36).

What is God's revelation? Mt presents God's will in five doctrinal blocks: (1) The Sermon on the Mount (Mt 5–7) gives the spirit needed to do God's will: dedication, internal and external, to God. (2) Mt 10 contains the marching orders for Christian convertmakers: nothing useless, total commitment, and single-mindedness. (3) In Mt 13, one aspect of the kingdom is described in parables: an external union, a Church, will spread. (4) Chapter 18 specifies the union of the members of the Church: Christians, who together form one family, must avoid scandal and forgive an erring member. (5) Mt 24 and 25 describe the fall of Jerusalem and foretell the end of the world. They teach victory to the persevering and punishment to the wicked.

In summary, these five doctrinal sections teach that the Christian, himself justified and internally dedicated to God (cf. also 15:1–20), must convert others, even the Gentiles (cf. 15:21–16:22) to God's kingdom, God's family, as he awaits the final day. This teaching is found in Jesus' Church. And this Church is founded on the rock, the man with the keys, the master of the beast of burden: Peter (16:13–20). Jesus' disciples must be willing to follow him, even to the cross (16:21–28), which will bring ultimate triumph (17:1–26).

Chapters 19–23 contain further details of God's will: divorce, clung-to wealth, and obstinate rejection of Jesus — all keep men from God's marriage feast, "For many are called, but few are chosen" (22:14). And during Jesus' life, the leaders had contemptuously refused his call. Mt 8:1–9:34 set forth many of Jesus' miracles in the presence of the Pharisees, who judged, "He is a tool of the archdemon; that is how he drives out demons!" (9:33 f.)

Mt's passion narrative describes the sufferings of God's spokesman and the rejection of him, the promised one of Israel. His resurrection is the victory of the king and assures the same to the citizens of his kingdom (Mt 26–28).

Mt has been partially summarized in 23:37:

> "Jerusalem Jerusalem! Murderess of prophets! Stoner of the messengers sent to you! How often have I been willing to gather your children as a mother bird gathers her brood under her wings! But you refused it! Mark well: you will find your house abandoned — a prey of desolation. Yes, I tell you, you will not see me again till you cry out: 'A blessing on him who comes in the name of the Lord!' "

The rest of Mt's teaching can be summarized by saying, "But my kingdom whose children need me, to whom I give my will, whose rulers are divinely sealed, and to whom I shall give eternal happiness is always open to you and to all, if only you would say, 'Blessed am I, your God!' "

Mt was meant primarily for Jews. Its teachings of God's will are taken by the Scribe from the storeroom — things old and new (cf. Mt 13:52). Earlier we called him a legalist, and that he is. His contribution to the synoptic mosaic of Jesus is Jesus, the royal lawgiver, revealer of God's will. All seek God's will. Here it is: Jesus is king and has revealed God's will. Keep it and it will keep you for eternity; this is the security of Mt!

With this general view of Mt's Gospel in mind, we can now examine in detail some representative passages.

THE MESSIAH'S BIRTH (Mt 1:18–25)

[18]Regarding the conception of Jesus Christ, the circumstances were as follows: His mother Mary had been espoused to Joseph; but before they lived together, it was found that she was pregnant by the holy spirit. [19]Joseph, her husband, being right-minded and unwilling to expose her, resolved to put her away without public formalities. [20]He had just made up his mind to this course when an angel of the Lord appeared to him in a dream and said: "Joseph, son of David, do not scruple to take Mary, your wife, into your home. Her conception was wrought by the holy spirit. [21]She will bear a son and you are to name him Jesus; for he will save his people from sins."[22]This event with all its circumstances was to fulfill the Lord's prediction made through the prophet, who says: [23]Behold! The virgin will be pregnant and give birth to a Son, who will be called "Emmanuel" — which means "God with us."

[24]After waking from his sleep, Joseph did as the angel of the Lord had directed him, and took his wife into his home. [25]He had no conjugal relations with her before she gave birth to a Son whom he named Jesus (1:18–25).

General context and literary form. From 1:18–2:23, Mt gives five stories: Jesus' birth, the Magi, the flight from Egypt, the slaughter of the Innocents, and the Nazarene. Whether these are "things that happened" or not is not the object of this commentary to discuss. Our concern is with what Mt is teaching. We think that he is teaching through the midrashic literary form. The midrash is a literary form which is a meditation on the Old Testament, seen in the light of a new insight, in the New Testament, caused by God's having become man. Midrash is not opposed to history. Whatever may be determined about the "things that happened," Mt is teaching, as we shall presently explain, his predominantly Jewish audience by these five stories that Jesus is the new Israel, the new David, and the new Moses. By implication, Jesus is also the new people, the new nation of Israel, the new kingdom of David, and the living law of Moses!

Our conclusion that Mt is teaching all of the above is based on the following summary of Mt's midrash with its Old Testament allusions:

1) First, there are indications that Mt teaches that Jesus is the new Israel. Before the reasoning here can be fully grasped, the Old Testament principle of interpretation called "solidarity" must be recognized. This means that the Semite identifies the individual and the group. One of the best Old Testament examples is Hos 11–14. There, the word "Jacob" is at one and the same time the person and the nation. Ephraim includes both the son of Joseph and the group of the northern tribes. Israel encompasses the man and the whole country. Now, to turn to the reasons we think Mt identifies Jesus as the new Israel, i.e., Jacob.

Jacob, the man, was from Abraham. When he returned from exile, he changed his name to Israel. The people Israel was to send forth a star to triumph over its enemies (Num 24:17 f.). In Egypt, the motley crew was delivered and made into God's own people, his "son." Its exile (721 B.C.) brought tears to its mother, Rachel.

Jesus was from Abraham (1:2–17). Jesus' star triumphed in homage and fear (2:1–12). He went into exile to avoid being killed (2:13–15). His mother, Rachel, mourned for those killed on the occasion of his exile (2:16–18). When he returned to the promised land, his name was the Nazarene (2:19–23). The Nazarene is the new Israel.

2) Jesus is the promised Davidic king. His father was Joseph, of the house of David (1:20). He is born of a virgin (1:23), the pleni-fulfillment of the 'almah, the queen-mother of Is 7:14. From Bethlehem, he will be the foretold ruler (2:1–6). Finally, he is the sprout of Jesse, David's father (2:19–23).

3) Jesus is the new Moses. Moses saved his people; Jesus is the Savior (1:22). The child of the bulrushes was saved from Pharoah; Jesus is saved from Herod (2:13–15). In exile, Moses had to wait until his enemies died; Jesus came back when his were dead (2:21). The new lawgiver has been born.

To detail all the reasons for all of these conclusions is beyond the scope of this work. One example is chosen in the following pages. We have chosen Mt 1:18–25 because it shows Jesus as one capable of revealing God's will — an important stone in Mt's contribution to the synoptic mosaic!

Summary of Mt's teaching in 1:18–25. Joseph's child is the Messiah. He, "God-with-us," is the fulfillment of the divinely promised Salvation by God.

Exegesis of 1:18–25.

1. (1:18a) *Regarding the conception of Jesus Christ, the circumstances were as follows.* Literally, the Greek reads: "Now (de) the generation of Jesus Christ was thus." We disagree with Fr. Kleist's translation and believe Mt is simply providing here a fitting title for this pericope.

2. (1:18b f.) *His mother Mary had been espoused to Joseph; but before they lived together, it was found that she was pregnant by the holy spirit. Joseph, her husband, being right-minded and unwilling to expose her, resolved to put her away without public formalities.*

Mt sets a problem, a conflict, before us. Joseph did not wish to meddle in God's affair, namely his betrothed's pregnancy.

a) The word "spirit" here, as in Mk 1:10 (cf. p. 10) means God's power. Many wish to excise the phrase, "by the holy spirit." It is genuine and should not be taken out of the text. There is no textual support for excising it. Those who wish to do so overlook its importance for Mt's teaching, i.e., that the child was God's affair and consequently Joseph did not wish to meddle.

b) Note well that the central person in this pericope is Joseph, not Mary or Jesus. These verses (18–25) thus finish the genealogy of 1:2–16.

c) *Joseph, being right-minded and unwilling to expose her, resolved to put her away without public formalities.* Two interpretations of this phrase are possible.

1) Joseph wished to put Mary away privately, not wishing to humiliate her. This interpretation understands the word *right-minded* (*dikaios*) to mean "kind," "charitable" toward Mary. It is easier to accept this interpretation if 1:18, "by the holy spirit" is considered a Matthean explanatory phrase or if it is excised.

On this interpretation it is also best to think that Joseph had some suspicions that Mary was an adultress.

2) The interpretation that the just Joseph thought Mary some sort of an adultress is *possible*, but hardly the more probable. We prefer St. Jerome's explanation that Joseph feared to intrude himself in God's work. Only such an explanation gives proper due to Joseph's holiness.

If Joseph had thought her an adultress, he had an obligation to expose her. Dt 22:23 f. says, "If within the city a man comes upon a maiden who is betrothed, and has relations with her, you shall bring them both out to the gate of the city and there stone them to death: the girl because she did not cry out for help though she was in the city, and the man because he violated his neighbor's wife. Thus shall you purge the evil from your midst." This law was still in force in contemporary Judea and Mt's usual meaning of "right-minded" or "just" is one who keeps God's law.

On the other hand, if Joseph thought her conception was from God, he had an apparent obligation to get out of God's way. The presupposition of this second interpretation is either a divine and partial illumination; or, by far the better, Joseph's undaunted faith in his wife. He would have reasoned, "Her pregnancy must be from God because she is so holy!" Such an act of charity is not beyond possibility in a man as holy as Joseph, the right-minded! Chapter 1:20 will bear out the possibility of this interpretation.

But both interpretations presuppose that the scene is statistical. And to decide the historicity of this scene is not our concern in this book. Mt is teaching that Joseph is holy, sublimely holy. We think that Mt is teaching that Joseph is so holy that he did not wish to meddle in God's work. "After all," Joseph reasoned, "no human can do anything but get in God's way in a circumstance where God may not want him."

3. (1:20–23) *He had just made up his mind to this course when an angel of the Lord appeared to him in a dream and said: "Joseph, son of David, do not scruple to take Mary, your wife,*

into your home. Her conception was wrought by the holy spirit.
She will bear a son and you are to name him Jesus; for he will
save his people from their sins." This event with all its circumstances was to fulfill the Lord's prediction made through the
prophet, who says: "Behold! The virgin will be pregnant and
give birth to a Son, who will be called Emmanuel — which means
'God with us.' "

The conflict had been presented in 1:18b f. Mt resolves it in
these verses. God gives Joseph permission to take the virgin-
mother as his wife, even though the spirit had caused her conception. The child will be the promised Savior of his own people,
God with them.

a) Both the angel of the Lord, a divine messenger, and the
dream are frequently found in the Old Testament to testify
to God's work. Son of David in reference to Jesus' father
is a confirmation of Mt 1:17 that Jesus is the promised son of
David.

b) Do not scruple to take Mary. . . . Her conception was
wrought by the holy spirit. Kleist's translation has omitted a par-
ticle (gar) which connects these two sentences. It means for or
you see, a conjunction expressing cause, inference, continuation,
or an explanation. Since we believe that both interpretations
given above under 1:18b are possible, this verse can take on two
meanings. A relevant rephrasing of 1:20b according to the first
interpretation would be: "Do not scruple (fear, literally) to take
Mary, for her conception has not been in adultery but by the
holy spirit." A comparable rephrasing in line with the second
interpretation would be, "Do not scruple (i.e., about Mary's
conception by the Holy Spirit) to take Mary." Here the second
sentence is an explanation of the first, removing the cause why
Joseph scrupled, i.e., to meddle in the spirit's affair of Mary's
conception. Whichever interpretation is preferred, there is no
doubt that Mt is teaching that the entire birth is God's affair.

c) You are to name him Jesus. It is noteworthy in Mt's
account Joseph names the child; in Lk 1:31, Mary is to do so.
There is no opposition, if the statistical is ignored and the teach-

ing of each is considered. Mt teaches Joseph's importance; the child is David's son!

Jesus etymologically means "Yahweh is salvation." Mt underlines the etymology by saying: *He will save his people from their sins.* The long-expected Savior has come. The object of his salvation is the sins of his own people, of Israel by first choice.

d) *The virgin will be pregnant.* In Is 7:14, the Hebrew word does not mean *virgin* in contemporary sense of the word. Mt, following the Greek translation of the Old Testament called the Septuagint, used the word for *virgin.* He is certainly teaching a virgin birth, although he does not stress the point.

e) *Emmanuel, God with us,* is emphatically brought out by Mt. It is a key to his good news. The news that God is with us — to save his people — almost begins Mt and does end it. In 28:18–20, Jesus initiates his new people by commissioning the baptizing of all nations and ends with the news that God is with us. "And mark: I am with you at all time as long as the world will last." From 1:25 and throughout the rest of his Gospel, Mt teaches what it means to have "God with us."

4. (1:24 f.) *After waking from his sleep, Joseph did as the angel of the Lord had directed him, and took his wife into his home. He had no conjugal relations with her before she gave birth to a Son, whom he named Jesus.*

Mt had presented the problem and its resolution. In these verses, he presents its result. Joseph, the father, takes the mother with no sexual relations and Jesus is born.

a) *Conjugal relations* is an excellent translation in this context of the Greek's literal, *did not know her.* The Hebrew notion of knowledge is never merely abstract, but some sort of activity. In the Old Testament when a man knows a woman, it frequently means to have intercourse with her.

b) *Before she gave birth to a son.* By "before" does Mt teach that Joseph and Mary had intercourse after Jesus' birth? If he does, he contradicts the Church's teaching that Mary was a virgin before, during, and after parturition.

The word "before" could have been used in this sentence to

mean that afterward Joseph and Mary had intercourse. It need
not, however, mean this. It can indicate no judgment on the
following period of time. Mt himself uses "until," "before" without meaning that afterwards the condition was changed. For
example, in 28:20, "I am with you at all times as long as the
world will last." (Cf. also Mt 12:20.) We therefore conclude
that Mt is here neither affirming nor denying Mary's virginity
after giving birth to Jesus.

Relating 1:18–25 to the entire Gospel of Mt. We said that
Mt will detail uniquely in the New Testament the revelation of
God's will. The man who dares reveal God's will must be God's
anointed. That Jesus was! His name, the spirit, his just Davidic
father, Yahweh's angel, the dream, and his virgin birth — all these
prove that he is God with us.

THE HAPPINESS OF THE MAN WHO NEEDS GOD
(Mt 5:1–12)

[1]One day when his eyes fell on the multitude, he went up a
mountainside, where he sat down, with his disciples close to him.
[2]Opening his lips he gave to his hearers a lengthy instruction,
saying:
[3]"Blessed are the humble souls,
    for theirs is the kingdom of heaven.
[4]Blessed are the meek and gentle,
    for they will inherit the land.
[5]Blessed are the sorrowing,
    for they will be consoled.
[6]Blessed are those who hunger and thirst after holiness,
    for they will be satisfied.
[7]Blessed are the merciful,
    for they will have mercy shown to them.
[8]Blessed are the singlehearted,
    for they will see God.
[9]Blessed are the promoters of peace,
    for they will rank as children of God.
[10]Blessed are the victims of persecution for conscience' sake,
    for theirs is the kingdom of heaven.
[11]Blessed are you when you are reviled, or persecuted,
    or made a target for nothing but malicious lies — for my sake.
[12]Rejoice; yea, leap for joy; a rich reward awaits you in heaven.
    So, too, were persecuted the prophets who preceded you."

General Context. Part of Mt's first doctrinal block is 5:1–12. The entire section includes Chapters 5 to 7. It is commonly called "The Sermon on the Mount." To understand any part of this unit, as all literature, it is necessary to have a fairly good grasp of the whole. Thus, we will give the student first a general outline of Chapters 5–7 and then briefly explain the spirit of the sermon.

Outline of Mt 5–7:

5:1 f.	Preparation for his words.
5:3–20	The Messianic new people. Its happiness. By its interior spirit, it fulfills God's will and thereby will enter life.
5:21–7:12	The New Doctrine.
5:21–48	The old and fulfilled law.
6:1–18	Old and "new" holiness.
6:19–7:12	New holiness.
6:19–24	Choice must be made: God or riches.
6:25–34	If God is chosen, all else comes.
7:1–5	Reasons for not condemning.
7:6–11	About holy things.
7:12	The norm of conduct: the golden rule.
7:13–23	The new promise.
7:24–27	Conclusion — security in his words.

Spirit of the sermon. Mt seemingly has in mind people who held three distinct and erroneous approaches to life and especially to God's law. The first are the Pharisees who do good for the wrong reason. The second are the Jewish teachers who were teaching the keeping of the law and its interpretation for its own sake. The third are antinomians who opposed any law and thought that spiritual gifts, not the keeping of an objective norm, were sufficient for salvation.

To oppose these three errors, Mt instills an approach to life which joins two delicately balanced principles. On the one hand, man must realize his sinfulness and admit his need for God. On the other hand, man must confess that all things are possible with Christ.

The sermon is then a concretized combination of: "If you will be my disciple, crucify yourself" (cf. Mt 16:24); and, "Without me, you can do nothing" (Jn 15:5).

The maxims found in the sermon are to be taken at their face value. The keeping of the humanly impossible task of loving God and our neighbor will be achieved by God. It is he who works both the willing and the doing (cf. Phil 2:13).

Literary form. In general, Chapters 5 — 7 are in the literary form of the Old Testament Wisdom books. Wisdom, for the Hebrew, was the right way of living. In particular, Chapters 5 — 7 contain proverbs and explanations of them. Proverbs are pithy sayings learned and proved from experience. Proverbs apply only to individual cases. They are not general norms.

Summary of Mt's teaching in 5:1–12. One who relies totally on God will be happy in the midst of any suffering. This joy is the right of anyone who lives the Christian life, i.e., of a member of the kingdom.

Exegesis of 5:1–12.

1. (5:1 f.) *One day when his eyes fell on the multitude, he went up a mountainside, where he sat down, with his disciples close to him. Opening his lips he gave to his hearers a lengthy instruction, saying*

In sum, Mt teaches in these two verses that large crowds were prepared to hear God's instructions from the Messiah. The Messiah too was ready to impart the divine will.

a) *He went up a mountainside.* Since Lk 6:17 says the sermon was delivered on a "level stretch," it is only sane exegesis to admit that we do not know the actual geographical location of the so-called "Sermon on the Mount."

If he did not intend to give us the geographical location of the sermon, what did Mt mean by "mountainside"? Mt uses the same phrase in 14:23 and the same idea in 17:11 and 18:16. In all the other cases, the mountainside is a place of privacy pervaded by an atmosphere of prayer or holiness. Here too, the mountainside is a place apart with a sacred atmosphere. It would be rather difficult to see, as some want, this mountain and Moses' "Mt. Sinai" as comparable, because the two incidents are distinct in their aspects. Mt 5 has none of the fearsome and majestic qualities that Ex 19–24 contains.

b) *He gave to his hearers a lengthy instruction.* Of interest to us is Jesus as teacher. Mt would literally be translated, *he was teaching (edidasken) them, saying.* . . . We think that Mt used *didaskō* in reference to Jesus, in order to describe him as the revealer of God's will. Our reasons are the following: (1) "To teach" (*didaskein*) appears 14 times in Mt; 8 times concerning Jesus' teachings, never with an object. (2) The rabbis were accustomed to teach the Torah, the Law. (3) The entire sermon is given in a context of Wisdom, i.e., the right way of living. (4) In Mt, Jesus teaches as fulfilling the Old Testament.

We therefore conclude that in Mt "to teach" is a technical phrase when predicated of Jesus. It means that Jesus is the One Teaching. He can uniquely reveal God's will for the right way of living. His revelation is no longer the Torah, but God's word! For us, a more meaningful phrase than "to teach" would be "Christ" or "Messiah" with the connotation of one who teaches God's will.

2. The Beatitudes. In summary, Mt's teaching in the beatitudes is the limitless amount of happiness of this new people who need God (5:3–12).

a) (5:3) *Blessed are the humble souls for theirs is the kingdom of heaven.* How wonderful that the great Christian Preacher spoke first of blessedness.

1) The word *blessed* comes from the Hebrew *ashre*, literally *happiness*. The term is common in the Hebrew Wisdom literature (cf. Pss 1:1; 32(33):1 f.; 118(119):1; Dan 12:12). It is very difficult to translate into English. The blessing (*bakar*) for the Hebrew was an internal spiritual energy given by Yahweh and certain to produce progeny, prosperity, and to give land. The "happinesses" result from the blessing.

Precisely how much in touch with reality are the beatitudes? St. Thomas, speaking ontologically, has said that happiness is the ultimate goal to which man by his nature tends. The existentialists would require joy to be appreciated only in the anguish of nothingness. Some men describe happiness as thinking pleasant thoughts a good deal of the time. The man who taught the beatitudes includes all of these concepts. He had profound insight when saying, "Oh the joys of the one who cannot be saddened by losing all apparent goods, and holds on to the One for whom he was made!" Dr. Victor E. Frankl of logotherapy fame would admit that such a one had found meaning for life.

St. Thomas says that the beatitudes correct the four false opinions about happiness; (a) happiness is found in affluence; by "blessed are the poor;" (b) happiness is in satisfying the appetite, whether irascible, concupiscible, or volitional; respectively corrected by, "blessed are the meek, the mourning, and those seeking justice." St. Thomas adds that earthly happiness is neither in moral virtues, nor in the active, nor in the contemplative life, but these are ways to God.

With St. Thomas and modern-day psychologists, Mt has written that earthly happiness is not something we can merit, but a state of mind. It is the state of mind of the poor, the needy, the one who yearns for God, because, having learned his nothing, he finds joy in his All!

2) *The humble souls.* The Greek reads literally, *the poor in spirit.* The Old Testament concept of the poor described originally those who had no money and could not withstand the oppression of the rich. By the time of the prophet, Zephaniah, the concept was taking on the notion of one who relied on God, i.e., who was needy, whether rich or poor, "For then I will remove from your midst the proud braggarts . . . . But I will leave as a remnant in your midst a people humble and lowly, who shall take refuge in the name of the Lord. They shall do no wrong and speak no lies; nor shall there be found in their mouths a deceitful tongue" (Zeph 3:11–14). The "in spirit" of "poor in spirit" strengthens the concept of the needy. In other words, the man poor in spirit *chooses* to need, to long for God.

For theirs is the kingdom of heaven. The kingdom of God and the kingdom of heaven are synonymous concepts. As we explained when we were discussing Mk 10:14 (cf. p. 25), God's kingdom is God's reign which will effectively bring about God's supernatural end. The man who refuses to need God thwarts this end, since he makes himself his own god. The poor, the needy, choose God and let God's kingdom have its sway.

The reign of the kingdom begins on earth. There is no reason to see the joys of the poor and their reception of the kingdom as belonging only to heaven. It is true that there is suffering as long as that for which the needy yearn is not totally and unloseably theirs. But the certainty of the possession lessens the sorrow and admits joy — now on earth! This joy to the poor is the keynote of the preacher's message to his new people.

b) (5:4)* *Blessed are the meek and gentle, for they will inherit the land.* This verse may be rephrased by "Oh, the amounts of happiness that will be to this new people who stand bent before God, for they will possess the new Promised Land."

1) *Meek and gentle* are Kleist's translation of the one Greek word *praeis*. The *praeis* are practically the same as the poor, the needy. The word may add to needy a notion of more experience of external difficulties. Thus, we have chosen to explain Kleist's "meek and gentle" by saying, "those who stand bent before God." They have suffered. As a result of their experience they choose God's will. Mt 11:29 predicates the same attribute of Jesus, "Take my yoke upon you and master my lessons, for I am gentle (*praus*, same root as *praeis*) and humble of heart."

2) *They will inherit the land.* The promised land of the Old Testament was Palestine. It was to be given to God's covenanted people, if they would keep the norms of the covenant. The new promised land is parallel to the kingdom of God in 5:3. In Hebrew poetry — of which the beatitudes are almost certainly an example — parallel phrases are also frequently synonymous concepts. Thus, "inherit the land," as God's kingdom, is not something geographical. It is rather a non-refusal of God's reign by

---

* In the best Greek manuscripts Mt 5:4 of Kleist's translation follows Mt 5:5. There is no textual evidence for omitting "Blessed are the meek and gentle, for they will inherit the land."

bending before God's will. As the needy, so the meek and gentle, i.e., those who bend before the continuous encounter with God, will be full of joy — come what may! The future tense of "will inherit the earth" does not indicate that the reward will be only in heaven. One reason for this is that there is no land in heaven to inherit.

With the explanations of 5:1–4 just given, we hope that the spirit of the beatitudes and the method of interpreting them, have been sufficiently laid before the reader. The rich hues of meaning in the Old Testament concept of the "poor" are explained in the other beatitudes. The promises contained in verses five to twelve are facets of the kingdom of God of 5:3. Therefore, we believe that you will, on reflection, be able to understand the following, brief rephrasing of the rest of the beatitudes. The shocking truth of life's reality is that if joy is not found in suffering through needing God, happiness will always disappear!

c) (5:5) *Blessed are the sorrowing, for they will be consoled.* Happy are those who weep, for they will be comforted! No cause of the weeping is given. God's will rarely comes under a religious guise. Whatever cause, the one who sorrows is close to needing God and capable of accepting the comfort of his often mysterious will. In other words, one who refuses is refusing the One causing sorrow.

d) (5:6) *Blessed are those who hunger and thirst after holiness, for they will be fully satisfied.* Happy are those who can be sated only by knowing, loving, and being loyal to God.

e) (5:7) *Blessed are the merciful, for they will have mercy shown to them.* Happy are those who practice the divine virtue of forgiveness, for to the extent they practice it, God will forgive them.

f) (5:8) *Blessed are the singlehearted, for they will see God.* Happy are those who give their innermost self to God. The singlehearted are totally dedicated to, and involved with, God and consequently give their "I" as much as possible to him. As a result, they receive him in his "I" as much as they are capable — here as well as in heaven.

g) (5:9) *Blessed are the promoters of peace, for they will rank as children of God.* Happy are those who strive to bring about the promised Messianic joy, i.e., total happiness (the Hebrew and Old Testament idea of *shalom, peace*). These are God's children, i.e., of God's nature. The new people of God will these peace-makers be.

h) (5:10) *Blessed are the victims of persecution for conscience' sake, for theirs is the kingdom of heaven.* Happy are those who endure suffering. They shall be under God's reign.

i) (5:11 f.) *Blessed are you when you are reviled, or persecuted, or made a target for nothing but malicious lies — for my sake. Rejoice; yea, leap for joy, a rich reward awaits you in heaven. So, too, were persecuted the prophets who preceded you.* Mt changes to direct address, "You." Happy, you, because of reviling, persecution, and calumny for the Messiah. Indeed, these are reasons for rejoicing, i.e., for Messianic exultation, since the reward is great afterwards, just as the prophets have received. When one becomes so needy of God and bent before his will as to accept even martyrdom, then one can be assured of experiencing God's reign in God's dwelling.

Relating 5:1–12 to the entire Gospel of Mt. The staid, stolid, secure-seeker, Mt is about to lay down God's law in the rest of 5 — 7. Its norms are demanding, more demanding than anyone can fulfill, "Be perfect as your heavenly Father" (5:48). One who chooses whatever God wills shall receive God's power, God's kingdom, shall be happy, so Mt begins his revelation of God's law to love him. Mt's picture of the Lawgiver Jesus of Nazareth begins with the paradox and shock that joy can be found in suffering, if one does not refuse God! It ends in a triumphant commander who rose from death!

THE MISSIONARY: HIS IRONIC SUFFERING, HIS NEED TO BE FEARLESS, AND HIS SANCTIONS (Mt 10:24–33)

[24]No pupil is above his teacher, and no slave above his master. [25]It is enough for a pupil to be treated like his teacher. If people called the head of the household "Beelzebul," how much more so the members of his family! [26]Therefore do not be afraid of

them. After all, nothing is concealed but must be made known some day. ²⁷What I tell you in the dark you have to speak out in broad daylight; and what you hear in a whisper you have to proclaim from the housetops. ²⁸And do not fear people that kill the body, but have no power to kill the soul; rather, fear him who has power to ruin both body and soul in the infernal pit. ²⁹Do not two sparrows sell for a penny? And yet, not one of them can drop dead to the ground without the consent of your Father. ³⁰As for yourselves, the very hairs on your head have all been numbered. ³¹Away, then, with all fear; you are more precious than whole flocks of sparrows.

³²In short, everyone who acknowledges me before the world will, in turn, be acknowledged by me before my Father in heaven; ³³but he who disowns me before the world will himself be disowned by me before my Father in heaven.

General context. Falling within the second general block of Mt's five large teaching sections is Mt 10:24–33. This second doctrinal grouping goes from 9:35 — 11:1. It is Mt's "Discourse on Missionary Activity." We shall give a general view of it in outline form and then summarize its spirit.

Outline:

9:35–10:4	Preparation. Jesus' love for people's salvation determines him to choose twelve helpers to whom he gives his power.
10:5–42	The body of the Discourse.
10:5–15	Rules: gratuitously work eschatological cures; proclaim God's kingdom only to Israel; take no provisions; etc.
10:6–33	Behavior in suffering: prudence; alert to godless; confidence; perseverence; flight; ironic suffering; be fearless; sanctions.
10:34–39	Choose suffering and the cross to gain life.
10:40–42	The worth of the disciples.
11:1	Conclusion.

Spirit of the Missionary Discourse. Mt applies his "poor in spirit" to missionaries. A missionary's effectiveness comes from God's power upon which he must rely.

Wherever, whenever, from whomever, and in whatever circumstances he encounters God, the missionary's response must be trust in God. The address is to "the twelve disciples" (10:1). We believe that from its content, the discourse is evidently meant for all of Mt's readers. Every Christian is a missionary by the very fact of being a Christian.

We have chosen 10:24–33 to bring out one aspect of the Matthean outlook on Christian life. For missionaries, Mt lays down some pithy norms. These norms are to bring a missionary to reliance on God. Mt tells what is God's will to be effective in spreading God's kingdom. Mt 10:24–33 is helpful in understanding Mt's general portrayal of Jesus, the monarch of the kingdom who is "God-with-us."

Literary form: a missionary discourse, that is, an orderly and extended expression of Mt's thoughts concerning how to spread God's kingdom effectively.

Summary of Mt's teaching in 10:24–33. The fact is that missionaries will suffer, with the most ironic persecutions. They should, nevertheless, be fearless in the face of persecution, slander, and even martyrdom. By courageously performing his missionary task, the Christian will be rewarded. Jesus will reciprocate the missionary's testimony to him.

Exegesis of 10:24–33.

1. (10:24 f.) *No pupil is above his teacher, and no slave, above his master. It is enough for a pupil to be treated like his teacher, and for a slave, like his master. If people called the head of the household "Beelzebul," how much more so the members of his family!* Irony of ironies! The very ones who come to save are called damnable. Mt has promised persecution in 10:16–23. He now turns to a particular twist of the suffering: like father, so son!

a) The only difficult word in these verses is *Beelzebul.* We find the word in the Old Testament. 2 Kg 1:2 ff., where in Hb, *ba'al zebub* is the god of the Philistine city, Ekron. The Old Testament is probably punning, changing a final letter "l" to "b." The Old Testament changes the god's name from the Philistine's

honorable title of "prince," or "lord of the earth" (from the
Ugaritic *ba'al zbl*) to the contemptuous "lord of the flies" (*ba'al-
zbb*). In the New Testament, the word, *beelzebul* is used syn-
onymously with master of the devils. Mt 12:24, "This man drives
out the demons merely as a tool of Beelzebul, the archdemon!"
(Cf. also Mk 3:22; Lk 11:15 ff.).

b) 10:24 f. teach then that, if Jesus was called the master of
devils, people will call his followers devils! If they crucified the
teacher and the master, the pupil and the slave will receive the
same!

2. (10:26 f.) *Therefore, do not be afraid of them. After all,
nothing is concealed but must be revealed some day. Nothing is
hidden but must be made known some day. What I tell you in
the dark you have to speak out in broad daylight; and what you
hear in a whisper you have to proclaim from the housetops.*

In sum, Mt teaches in these verses that the missionaries are
to be fearless. Despite the persecution and slander that will
come, all will be revealed. Jesus' message, his goodness, and theirs
will out. As a result, fearlessly publish, *speak out in broad daylight, proclaim from the housetops* the Word who had been
hidden during Jesus' lifetime. As we shall see in Mt 13, God's
word is like a seed, a leaven; it will be effective. The missionary
needs but rely on God and fearlessly proclaim God's word. Mt
here applies his, "Let your first concern be the kingdom of God
and what he requires of you; then you will have all these things
thrown in for good measure" (6:33).

3. (10:28–31) *And do not fear people that kill the body, but
have no power to kill the soul; rather, fear him who has power to
ruin both body and soul in the infernal pit. Do not two sparrows
sell for a penny? And yet, not one of them can drop dead to the
ground without the consent of your Father. As for yourselves, the
very hairs on your head have all been numbered. Away, then, with
all fear; you are more precious than whole flocks of sparrows.*

Mt continues his injunction to be fearless. Even when the missionaries face bodily martyrdom, let them be fearless. Real life is
the important thing. Only God can send the whole person to

Gehenna (Kleist: *infernal pit*; cf. next paragraph). Therefore, fear God? No, do not even fear him. If he protectingly cares for a worthless bird and is lovingly concerned with your hair, how much more your whole person!

a) The *infernal pit* is a good English rephrasal of Gehenna. The name "Gehenna" refers originally to a valley west of Jerusalem where infants were sacrificed to the god Moloch (cf. Jer 7:31; 9:5; 39:35). King Josiah used the same valley to burn offal. The term is frequent in rabbinical literature of the first century A.D., where it refers to the place of punishment of the evil.

In the New Testament, this last meaning of a place of punishment has been brought over, with all the apocalyptical (cf. p. 74 f.) symbolism attached to it. The eternity of the punishment in the philosophical sense of ceaseless change and duration is not found in the Bible. The notion of an indefinitely extended time (*aiōn*) is found in the New Testament and is predicated of the punishment of the afterlife. "But if your own hand or foot tempts you to sin, cut it off and throw it away; it is better for you to enter life crippled or lame than to keep both hands or both feet and be consigned to the everlasting (*aiōnion*) fire" (Mt 18:8). Therefore, there is a basis in the New Testament for the later philosophical understanding of punishment in the afterlife as a condition which is everlasting and unalterable.

In sum, then, the ceaseless burning of offal in Gehenna is a symbol for punishment. Through later understanding, it was seen as eternal punishment.

b) From Kleist's translation of 10:28–31, one might understand a dichotomy in the human being, i.e., a two-part "body" and "soul." Not until the book of Wisdom about 150 B.C. did the Jew come to an inkling of the two-part distinction in the human. Until then, the human was a whole. The distinction never became too popular and, even in these verses, we believe that a different translation would be better. The word translated "soul" is *psychē* in Greek which is from the Hebrew *nephesh*. In the Old Testament *nephesh* normally means the whole person as strong or living. The word translated "body" is *sōma*, from the

Hebrew *guph*. This normally means the whole person as weak or dead.

The best translation, then, of the very Semitic Mt would run in 10:28, "Do not quake before those who can take life from the body (*sōma*), but cannot annihilate the life itself (*psychē*). Fear rather him who can plunge both body and its life into Gehenna." Mt confirms our interpretation in 10:31, "You (not "your soul") are more precious than whole flocks of sparrows!" The whole person is precious, not just the body or just the soul. Courage and trust in the Almighty to save the entire "I."

4. (10:32 f.) *In short, everyone who acknowledges me before the world will, in turn, be acknowledged by me before my Father in heaven; but he who disowns me before the world will himself be disowned by me before my Father in heaven.*

In 10:32 f. Mt tells the sanction of a missionary. Testimony for testimony; acknowledgment for acknowledgment! By performing his duty in the face of suffering caused by the godless, the missionary will be rewarded. Jesus will reciprocate his testimony before the Father. But the same follows for those who refuse to bear witness to Christ.

The Hebrew never saw knowledge, acknowledgment, as a merely passive and abstract concept. We saw this in explaining Mt 1:25. Here too, "to acknowledge" Jesus means to bear witness, to spread the kingdom, to love him as a missionary. When the missionary's time for judgment comes, Jesus will acknowledge him, witnessing to the Father on his behalf. Paul has given the best commentary on the hope a Christian may have, "Who shall make accusation against the elect of God? It is God who sanctifies! Who shall condemn? It is Christ Jesus who died, yes, and who rose again, who is at the right hand of God, who also interceded for us!" (Rom 8:34).

Relating 10:24–33 to the entire Gospel of Mt. In Mt Jesus is primarily the King who has begun the kingdom. Members must be brought into the kingdom. Every member has an obligation to bring others to Christ. But on whom should he rely? Being poor and needy, a Christian will be relying only on God — come what suffering may. As a result, he will be fearless in proclaiming the King. His reward, because God is with him, will be his entire person's entrance into the domain of Jesus' Father.

THE JOY THAT FINDING THE KINGDOM GIVES (Mt 13:44).

The kingdom of heaven reminds me of a treasure buried in the field: as soon as a person discovers it, he hides it again, and off he goes in his joy and sells all his possessions and buys that field.

In explaining this verse, our method of procedure will be to give its general context, its literary form, and its exegesis. Under general context, we shall outline 13:1–52, explain the word "parable," distinguish our aim from a statistical one, give the spirit of the parables, tell their purpose in Mt as distinct from Jesus' or Mark's use, and finally explain why we chose 13:44.

General context.

Outline:

13:1–52	The reason for "parables" and why men should join the Church.
13:1–35	God's merciful fulfillment of a prophecy.
13:1–9	"Parable" of the Sower.
13:10–23	Two results of the "parables": mercy and more explanation.
13:24–30	"Parable" of the weeds.
13:31 f.	The mustard seed: God's kingdom is effective even though puny in its start.
13:33	The leaven: nothing can stop God's effective kingdom.
13:34 f.	Fulfillment of the psalm.
13:36–52	Even though there are evil men in the Church, it is worth any sacrifice to enter it.
13:36–43	God's kingdom: a visible union of men to endure to the end of time to bring the good to heaven.
13:44	The joy that finding it gives.
13:45 f.	Worth all the treasury of a rich man.

13:47–50   A visible union of men to endure until the end of
            the world, when its evil members will be punished.
13:51 f.   One who understands Jesus' teaching has the right
            to teach the old and new revelation.

Definition of "parable." A glance at the preceding outline
shows how important it is to understand the word "parable."
Any interpretation of chapter thirteen flows from the concept of
"parable." Too, Mt 13 contains seven "parables": the sower,
mustard seed, weeds, leaven, treasure, pearl, and net. Webster
defines a parable as a "usually short fictitious story that illus-
trates a moral attitude or a religious principle." The parable must
be carefully distinguished in this terminology from an allegory,
any of whose points teach.*

The Greek word *parabolē* as found in the New Testament does
not maintain Webster's restricted definition for the English
"parable." It is not correct, therefore, merely to transliterate the
word. In fact, it may mean "comparison" (Lk 5:36; Mk 3:23);
"symbol" (Heb 9:9; 11:19); "proverb" (Lk 4:23; 6:39); "riddle"
(Mk 7:17); or "rule" (Lk 14:7), and so forth. This is not unexpected when we consider the Semitic background of the New
Testament. *Parabolē* translates the Hebrew word *mashal*. *Mashal*
includes all the distinctions we Westerners make between parable, proverb, riddle, allegory, fable, jest, and many more.

How then, ought we to define the biblical word translated
"parable"? We cannot generalize. Each figure of speech has to be
understood in its own phrasing, context, and explanation by its
author.

Matthean "parable" vs. Jesus' use. In our preface, we mentioned that the purpose of this book would be to try to find the
literal sense of God's inspired word, not to find the "thing that

---

* Recently Scripture scholars have added a new element in the definition
of a parable by acknowledging that a parable must have some allegorizing
points. We prefer in this text to keep Webster's definition when discussing
a true parable. We readily admit that few New Testament parables are true
parables according to Webster's definition, i.e., figures which contain only
one teaching. But, for a parable with allegorical elements, we prefer the name
allegorized parable or parabolical allegory — depending on which literary
form predominates.

happened." This principle applies to the use of "parable" also. It is an absorbing and educating study to try to learn what a particular "parable" meant in the mouth of Jesus. It is an exciting and inspiring insight to find the particular life-situation (*Sitz im Leben*) in which Jesus first pronounced each separate "parable." But results are at worst educated guesses and at best give moral certainty that Jesus spoke the parables. But searching out the meaning of a parable in the sense intended by Matthew (or Mark or Luke) in the particular context of his Gospel teaches us God's inspired word.

Therefore, a "parable" may not be generalized out of the particular teaching of Mt, Mk, or Lk. "Many are called, but few are chosen" is applied by none of the evangelists to religious vocations, though it is by many novice masters. Too, the same "parable" may be used by the same author in two contexts with two meanings. Any proverb admits that! But it does not follow because a "parable" fits a particular situation today, that the meaning is inspired by God. Such an interpretation is neither more nor less than an accommodation. It is not a meaning of God.

In sum, then, when reading the Gospels, we will be looking for the meaning of "parable" in the individual evangelist, not in the life of Jesus. Our result will be the meaning of God's inspired word. Since we have chosen to study Mt 13:44, we will later have to determine the individual literary form of this "parable" to learn what Mt teaches in these verses.

The spirit of the "parables" as used by Mt. Mt uses the "parables" to show the difference in understanding Jesus' message on the part of the disciples and on the part of the people of Israel. Too, the "parables" cause a difference in understanding even in the disciples.

The people of Israel show obduracy in the face of the "parables." As Mt 13:35 says: "Thus the prophecy of Isaiah is more and more fulfilled in them. It says: 'Your ears will hear, yet you will not understand; your eyes will look, yet you will not see. For blunted is the sense of this people: their ears are hard of hearing, and their eyes are shut; thus neither their eyes see, nor their ears hear, nor their minds understand and they are not converted and healed by me.' "

But even among the disciples, there will be the good and the bad (13:24–30; 13:36–43). Mt's "parables" are thus used to show the difference in understanding of those who hear the Word in the words about the kingdom.

As is evident from the results of the understanding, the "parables" in Mt 13 are both ecclesiastical and eschatological. They are ecclesiastical, for the response to the "parables" has already divided a visible union of men, a Church, from Israel. They are eschatological, i.e., containing the final times. This is true, because, based on the response to the "parables," an ultimate finality is awaited which will further divide the disciples who are within the Church.

The concept of "understanding" is vital for the interpretation of Mt's parables. "Understanding" (sunienai) is one of the three qualities which make up a Matthean disciple of Christ. The other two are faith (pistis) and need (mikros). Faith is trust or obedience, especially in God's fatherly kindness and Jesus' power. Needy, a disciple must choose to be lacking, empty, in order to receive from God.

Of special interest to us in chapter thirteen of Mt is "understanding." Its act is both volitional and intellectual. As volitional, it is a willingness of the human to grasp God's word. As intellectual, it is a divine gift of perception. The content of this understanding is God's Word, especially as found in the word of the kingdom. A disciple may be found lacking in it but only temporarily; if he lacks it completely, he ceases being a disciple. The contrary of understanding is obduracy.

We can now state more precisely the spirit of the Matthean "parables." It is a willingness to perceive, and a divine gift of perceiving, The Word as found in the words about God's kingdom. Its result is to distinguish both disciples among themselves and disciples from those outside the Church.

When the spirit of the Matthean "parables" is known, we can explain more fully that in Mt's Gospel we are speaking neither of Jesus' use of the parables, nor Mk's. In Jesus' life, the parables were his response to a particular crisis which effected mercy in those who received them and allowed those who did not receive them to condemn themselves. In Mk, they are an act of God's condemnation: "To you the secret of the kingdom of God has been given; but to those who are outside everything comes by way of the parables, *so that* (as Scripture says) they may look, but see nothing; they may hear and hear, but understand nothing; *otherwise they might turn to God and* be forgiven" (Mk 4:11 f. *New English Bible.* My italics). Mt's "parables" teach a division already present. Mk's condemn. Jesus used them to show mercy and permit people to condemn themselves.

We chose Mt 13:44 first, because it is short enough to allow us to concentrate on the background principles needed to understand all the parables, especially of Mt. Second, Mt 13:44 shows the positive response of one who has understanding. It thereby catches the positive side of the spirit of Mt's parables. Third, 13:44 is a literary model of "parable."

Literary form of Mt 13:44: a simile or a comparison. It would seem that the comparison is explicitly expressed in 13:44, since the verse begins, "The kingdom is like . . ." (Kleist, "The kingdom of Heaven reminds me . . ."). No great stress can be laid on the distinction between a simile and comparison, however. The reason is that the "like" may be a Matthean Semitism which means no more than "It is the case with . . ." and leaves unknown whether the comparison is expressed or not. What is the point of the simile or comparison? To that we shall return under the exegesis below.

We said that this parable was a model of parables. The reason is that no matter what type of figure a teacher uses, he wishes it easily memorable. The best aid to memory is daily experience with an exciting twist or ending. Both daily experience and a twist are found in this parable. Every man who has ever strolled a street knows what it is to see something bright, the hope that this bright object is valuable, and the resulting joy if the value is great. Our parable envisions a man who farms or digs for a

living. How great his joy, if he finds the hard object his pick has
struck to be a treasure. All Palestinians had a hope of finding such
a treasure. They knew of centuries of invasions which had forced
their Israelite ancestors to hide jars of silver coins or jewels, and
the Matthean audience could feel the anticipation and joy of
the worker. Mt 25:25 says in a situation similar to that of
former Israelites, "So I shrank from doing anything at all and
went to bury your talent in the ground."

Exegesis of 13:44.

*The kingdom of heaven reminds me of a treasure buried in the
field: as soon as a person discovers it, he hides it again, and off
he goes in his joy and sells all his possessions and buys that field.*

We believe the point of the comparion of this "parable" is
the joy of the finder. It is neither the hiddenness of God's
kingdom, its incomparable worth, nor the "heroism" of the man
in selling all he has in order to buy the field.

The point of the comparison could not be the hiddenness
of God's kingdom. In context of this parable it would lead to the
ridiculous teaching that if you happen to stumble on the kingdom, you can buy it. This teaching would be contrary to the
New Testament doctrine that the kingdom is a gift. Surely, the
kingdom is hidden, but that is not the point here.

Nor is the point of comparison that the kingdom is the treasure,
i.e., its incomparable worth. It would follow that heaven could
be purchased. Heaven or God's kingdom is not for sale — no
matter how much or how little we give up.

Too, one may not seek a teaching about the injustice of a
man who buys property of greater known value. The entire New
Testament as well as Mt condemns injustice. The finding, hiding,
and buying are all part of the story, not part of Mt's teaching.

Finally, there is little "heroism" in investing all my possessions
in a solid bargain. While it is true that a "bird in the hand" but
"pig in a poke" are excellent proverbs, they are not within the
ambit of this parable. Thus, the parable is not teaching heroic
poverty nor trust in God's kingdom.

The point of the parable is *in his joy*. The first and best reason that this is the point of the "parable" is that there is nothing left which could be the point. In the preceding paragraphs, we have removed all other possibilities.

A second reason which confirms our interpretation is Mt's juxtaposition of 13:44 and 13:45 f. The next verses run, "Again, the kingdom of heaven reminds me of a merchant in quest of beautiful pearls: as soon as he discovers one pearl of great value, off he goes and promptly sells all his possessions and buys it." True, in this second parable, the joy is not expressed. True, too, this second "parable" more readily lends itself to a comparison of an incomparable buy. The "buy," however, is precisely what is against this interpretation.

We believe that the two parables complement each other and that is Mt's reason for putting them side by side. We would surmise the process of joining 13:44 and 13:45 f. to be as follows. Mt found two pre-existing "parables." The first parable (13:44) contained an explicit note of joy. The second parable (13:45 f.) contained the story of a rich merchant who surrendered a fortune for a specially great pearl. If the two are juxtaposed, Mt reasoned, the great joy of God's kingdom will be taught by each. As Joachim Jeremias has haid, "The decisive thing in the twin parable is not what the two men give up, but the reason for their doing so: the overwhelming experience of the splendour of their discovery."

Relating 13:44 to the entire Gospel of Mt. Mt's "happinesses" began his Sermon on the Mount. We find the overpowering joy of the kingdom once again taught in the simple and memorable parable of the hidden treasure. Once grasped, the kingdom causes such joy that the poverty, dedication, and total surrender in loving God's living kingdom are of no count. We have seen the King, God-with-us, the missionary's reliance, and once again its joy. Mt's fundamental principles of Jesus as God's King who brings God's kingdom are perfected by the joy experienced under his reign.

LIMITLESS FORGIVENESS (Mt 18:21–35).

21Then Peter came up and said to him: "Lord, how many times may my brother wrong me and still claim my pardon? As many as seven times?" 22"No," Jesus replied: "I do not say, 'as many as seven times,' but 'as many as seventy times seven!' 23That is why the kingdom of heaven reminds me of an earthly king who, once upon a time, desired to settle accounts with his officials. 24In the course of the settlement one who owed him ten thousand talents presented himself; 25and since he had no means of paying, the master ordered him to be sold with wife, children, and all he had, and payment to be made. 26Then the official went down on his knees and, prostrating himself before him, said 'Have patience with me, and I will pay you everything.' 27Touched to the heart, the master of that official canceled his debt and set him free. 28But no sooner had that official gone outside than he met one of his fellow officials who owed him a hundred denarii; and, grasping him, he was about to choke him, saying: 'Pay what you owe.' 29Then his fellow official went down on his knees and pleaded with him: 'Have patience with me and I will pay you.' 30But he would not hear of it; on the contrary, he went and had him thrown into prison until he should pay the amount owed. 31Naturally, his fellow officials, who saw what had happened, were deeply grieved; and they went to their master to tell him all that had taken place. 32Then the master summoned him 'You merciless man,' he said to him: 'I canceled that whole debt of yours because you pleaded with me. 33Was it not proper for you, too to take pity on your fellow official just as I had taken pity on you?' 34And with indignation his master turned him over to the jailers until such time as he should pay the whole debt. 35In the same way my heavenly Father will treat you if you do not each forgive your brother from your heart.

General context. Mt 18:21–35 falls within the fifth part of Mt's Gospel, The Way toward Suffering. The first section from 16:21–18:35 deals with the disciples' preparation. The particular division within which 18:21–35 falls is the Christian family as avoiding scandal, trying to convert a sinner, and using mercy as its norm.

Outline of 18:1–35: The qualities of the members of the King's family.

18:1–5   The "greatest" disciple is the neediest. One who welcomes him welcomes Christ.

18:6–20	True brotherhood.
18:6–9	Care to avoid scandal.
18:10–14	The high value of a brother.
18:15–20	A sinning brother, even though he refuses all admonition, may be won back by the community's effective prayer.
18:21–35	How much forgiveness? Limitless!

Spirit of 18:21–35. The third great block of Mt's teaching, Chapter 18, considers the kingdom as a family. "How should brothers treat one another?", is the query implicit in Chapter 18. The answers to this question give the spirit of this chapter. Negatively, avoid scandal. Positively, appreciate the value put on your brother by God since God has given his own messenger to him and since God searches after him as a divine shepherd. As a result, do all to gain back a brother who may sin; especially, forgive him. Therefore, the spirit of Chapter 18 is the relationship found within a family. Chapter 18:21–35 the spirit of a family to the virtue of forgiveness. Blood is thicker than water — unless the water allows us to see a fellow Christian as a brother.

Literary form of 18:21–35. Just as in 13:44, we have the expression of a simile or comparison in 18:23, literally: "The kingdom of heaven is like . . . ." The literary form seems to be partially a parable in the technical sense, i.e., a story with one teaching, and partially allegory. The one teaching essential to the parable is evident: limitless forgiveness. The allegorizing elements are in brief: (1) The king is God; (2) the servants are two members of the Church; (3) 10,000 talents is an unimaginably great amount; (4) 100 denarii, a comparable pittance. We shall return to these identifications in the exegesis.

Exegesis of 18:21–35.

1. (18:21) *Then Peter came up and said to him, "Lord, how many times may my brother wrong me and still claim my pardon? As many as seven times?"*

a) A Westerner may think that Peter is being rather niggardly,

especially if the reader has gone to confession often. But for the
Semite, the number "seven" is a perfect number. Ever since
the book of Genesis the Bible uses seven to mean "totality,
fullness, or completeness." We do not know the source from which
this number received this signification. But then, we use the
number thirteen to mean bad luck and I, for one, do not know
the origin of this. I accept its meaning and joke about it, as part
of our culture. Do not belittle Peter's query. He was being
extremely generous. He was asking, "Should one forgive a perfect
number of times?"

b) There is something pathetic in putting this question into
Peter's mouth. Mt wrote many years after Peter's denial. Of all
people of all time who had experienced a perfect forgiveness,
Peter will always stand as the example.

2. (18:22) *"No," Jesus replied; "I do not say, 'as many as
seven times,' but 'as many as seventy times seven!'"* Jesus' rule
for forgiveness, in typical Oriental exaggeration, brings out the
limitless number of times. Take a perfect number (seven), multi-
ply it ten times over (seventy), and then remultiply it by the
perfect number it is! Of course, one is not to come up to the
number 490. The teaching is a limitless amount of times.

Too, the number chosen seems to be an echo of the vengeance
of Lamech in Gen 4:23 f., "Ada and Sella, hear my voice, wives
of Lamech, give ear to my speech: I kill a man for wounding
me, a youth for bruising me. If Cain shall be avenged sevenfold, Lamech seventy times sevenfold." Lamech "outcained" the
fratricidal Cain, so Christians should better Lamech's vengeance
in forgiving — limitlessly.

3. (18:23–35) These verses are an allegorized parable which
applies the norm of 18:22. This parable teaches that forgiveness
of the brothers should be similar to the limitless, easily obtained
mercy of God; if not they shall have to pay an eternal debt.
It therefore applies the rule stated in 18:22, "seventy times seven."

a) (18:23) *That is why the kingdom of heaven reminds me
of an earthly king who, once upon a time, desired to settle
accounts with his officials.*

As we shall see, this "parable" is not too farfetched for the absolute Roman reign of the day. The details that are stretched out of reality are precisely those which are allegorized. The beginning of the picture takes for granted a king whose kingdom stretches throughout a far-flung area. The king decides to call in the accounts of all the royal officials.

b) (18:24) *In the course of the settlement one who owed him 10,000 talents presented himself.* One of the royal officials is of such stature that he had control of revenues totalling up to 10,000 talents. The fluctuation both of the dollar and the talent prohibits any precise evaluation of this figure. It is enough to say that the amount was unimaginably immense. It may have run as high as $20,000,000 and is one of the details stretched out of reality. The reason that 10,000 and talents were chosen is that they were the highest amount of reckoning in those days. In the United States of a few years ago, a million was about the highest number used. Today, a billion is spoken of frequently. In a few years, the number trillion may be common parlance. The point is that this official owed an amount that never could be paid.

c) (18:25) *Since he had no means of paying, the master ordered him to be sold with wife, children, and all he had, and payment be made.* This cannot be allegorized to indicate God's justice, for example. One reason is that the amount which would be accrued would be infinitesimally below that needed for payment. Also, personal, not familial responsibility, is the object of justice. Rather, the wrath of the master is part of the picture which strongly limns the king's great mercy in the following verses.

d) (18:26) *Then the official went down on his knees, and, prostrating himself before him, said: "Have patience with me, and I will pay you everything."* The description is of most profound humiliation. No one can do more than grovel, knee to the ground, before another human. Actually, of course, there was no hope that the official could reimburse such a debt. But the man was begging, with every pretext for life — for himself and his.

e) (18:27) *Touched to the heart, the master of that official canceled his debt and set him free.* The master gave more than was asked: cancellation and freedom.

f) (18:28 f.) A similar picture is painted between the same official and one of his underlings. The amount involved is 100 denarii. Again, due to fluctuations, no precise sum can be determined. A fair guess can be made that a denarius was the amount made by a common laborer for one day's work (cf. Mt 20:1–16). At any reckoning, it was incomparably less than the higher official had just been forgiven. Too, it could have been repaid. Yet forgiveness was refused!

g) (18:30–34) The king is informed. He, in turn, urges the previous debt. It would not be right to read injustice into the story, saying that the debt had already been canceled and no one should go back on his word. That reasoning just doesn't belong to the "parable." This "parable's" teaching is not fear that God's word of forgiveness may be changed. It is teaching God's great mercy in forgiving and a Christian's need to forgive.

h) (18:35) *In the same way my heavenly Father will treat you if you do not each forgive your brother from the heart.* In a sentence, the entire allegorized parable is summed up. The story is an excellent picture of the Our Father's, "Forgive us our trespasses, as we forgive those who trespass against us." Mercy requires love. Love should be part of the familial kingdom of the Church, so Mt 18 teaches. Where it is lacking, God's mercy too must of necessity be lacking. His mercy is willing to forgive sin, an unimaginably great debt. Our love toward a brother should be willing to forgive any debt, a comparably trivial matter!

Relating 18:21–35 to the entire Gospel of Mt. We said that the king and the kingdom are the fundamental principles of Mt. Here, the members of the kingdom can participate in the king's quality of mercy. "God-with-us," even to dying for us, he is our king. Paradoxically, the king came to forgive sins! Mt 18:21–35 teaches how we should imitate the king, in our own relations to our brothers, "Forgive us, as we forgive."

THE PAROUSIA WILL BE UNEXPECTED AND SUDDEN. THEREFORE WATCH!
(Mt 24:36–42).

[36]"But, regarding the day and hour, no one knows, not even the angels in heaven, nor yet the Son, but only the Father. [37]As it was in the days of Noah, so it will be at the advent of the Son of Man: [38]in the days preceding the flood, people went on eating and drinking, marrying and giving in marriage, till the day when Noah entered the ark; [39]and they suspected nothing till the flood came and swept them all away. So it will be at the advent of the Son of Man. [40]At that moment, if two are in the field, one may be taken up and one abandoned; [41]if two women are grinding with the handmill, one may be taken up and one abandoned. [42]Keep awake, therefore; you do not know on what day your Lord returns."

General context. These verses fall within the seventh part, teaching The End and the Fulfillment, which goes from 24:1–28:20. The pericope we have chosen falls within the unit which 24:1 — 25:46 makes. An outline of it and its spirit will be given in the following:

Outline of 24:1–2:46. Victory to the persevering. Punishment to the wicked. Suffering for all.

24:1–25:30	The unimaginable sufferings will make even some disciples fall.
24:1–14	Salvation will be for those whom the calamitous sorrows do not cause to loves less.
24:15–20	The sorrow which will be caused by the fulfillment of Daniel's prophecy when Jerusalem is sacked.
24:21–31	Let not the Christians be deceived. Jesus' apocalyptically described Parousia will be unannounced, even though unique sufferings and false prophets will precede it.
24:32–35	The signs of the one coming are recognizable, in this generation's lifetime. His coming is more certain than the eternal symbol's continuing. This coming is the Fall of Jerusalem.

24:36–25:30   The time of his other coming (the Parousia) will be unexpected and sudden.

25:31–46   The reward for acts of charity done to Jesus will be eternal life. The punishment for omitting these acts of charity will be eternal suffering.

Spirit of 24:1–25:46. The spirit of this entire discourse is one of mystery and of certainty. The mystery is based on lack of knowledge as to when the end will come. The certainty is that Christ will return in glory and that Christians know how to conduct themselves as they await his coming. The sign certifying his return was the fall of Jerusalem.* The certain way to act in these eschatological times is by trust shown in acts of love.

Literary form of apocalypse. There is no single literary form found in 24:36–42. Therefore, we will have to detail the literary form of each section in our exegesis.

However, the literary form called "apocalyptic" is important for an understanding of these verses as well as all of Chapters 24 and 25 and their parallels in the other Synoptics. Therefore, we wish to discuss this form here.

The apocalyptic literary form is that literary form which teaches hope through past history, couching its message in a strange (to us) use of symbols, enigmatic numbers, pseudonyms, and catastrophic happenings. This literary form was common among extra-biblical writings, e.g., *The Assumption of Moses, Book of Enoch, Testament of the Twelve Patriarchs,* and others. It is also common enough in the Bible, e.g., the book of Revelations or the Apocalypse; parts of Daniel; Ezekiel; Mk 13:24–27; Mt 24:29–31; Lk 21:25–28.

The apocalyptical form began around 200 B.C. The psychological origin of the apocalyptical literary form seems to have been: (1) a disillusionment brought about by the slowness of the golden era which was expected to follow the return from exile;

---

* There is a dispute among scholars whether Mt was written before or after A.D. 70 the date of the fall of Jerusalem. We prefer a date after A.D. 70. For more confirmation cf. A. Wikenhauser, *New Testament Introduction* (New York: Herder and Herder, 1962), pp. 195–197; *Peake's Commentary,* No. 673, j and k.

(2) a lack of prophets, i.e., men who declared God's will; (3) a need to continue hoping; (4) and, a need to hide the spirit of hope from foreign oppressors. Thus, the Old Testament apocalypses satisfied a need to continue hoping in God's promises. The New Testament writers used this pre-existing literary mold to teach hope when Christians felt the uncertainty of the time of the second coming of Christ. It was the way they knew to express hope and hide their hope from the Romans. It was as natural for them to use the apocalyptic form as for you or me to write a letter to carry a message.

One of the most important results of seeing this literary form in parts of Mt 24–25 is that one will not press the details of an apocalyptically described event. Extra-biblical sources contain many of the details which Mt has in 24:29–31: "Directly after the distress of those days, the sun will darken, the moon cease to shed her light, and the stars fall from heaven. The foundations of the universe will rock. And then the sign of the Son of Man will appear in the sky, and then all the tribes of the earth will lament when they see the Son of Man riding the clouds overhead with great might and majesty. And he will send his angels sounding a mighty trumpet, and they will assemble his elect from the four winds, from one edge of the horizon to the other." Since, as was said, many of the details in these verses are found outside the Bible, we must grant either that God gave the gift of foretelling divine and future events to many or that we have here a common method of expressing a catastrophic happening. The latter alternative is the more likely. Therefore, the only history foretold (that is, an event which will happen) by these symbols is that there will be an end. We may also safely conclude that Mt did not know any signs of its coming. We are not even certain precisely what the sign of the Son of Man in the sky will be. In the middle of an apocalyptic section, no precise value of the symbol should be attempted.

One of our reasons for choosing 24:36–42 was to be able to discuss the apocalyptic literary form. About six chapters of the Synoptics become well-nigh unintelligible without knowing the principles of interpreting that literary form. Another reason we chose 24:36–42 was to introduce an important concept called the "Parousia." A third reason was to bring out the Synoptic's teaching on being prepared. The final reason was to give some examples where exegetes are not convinced of the precise meaning of some verses.

Exegesis of 24:36–42.

1. (24:36) *"But regarding that day and hour, no one knows, not even the angels in heaven, nor the Son, but only the Father."* The literary form of this verse is that of a "saying." Its teaching, in summary, is that the "Parousia" must be unexpected, because only the Father knows its date.

a) Mt in 24:29–35 had been speaking of a second and definitive coming of Christ. This day, so certain to come and so uncertain as to time, has been titled the "Parousia."

What is the Parousia? When was it expected? When will it come? The Parousia is a technical term referring to the coming of our Lord at the end of time. Etymologically, it means "being along side of; presence; coming; arrival." It is a fit name for the Presence, that is, the second and definitive coming of Jesus. The Parousia will be the final act of the eschatological times which we mentioned in explaining Mk 1:9. At the Parousia, Christ will show the holiness of the elect and will punish the evil.

When was the Parousia expected? In general, the New Testament authors seem to expect the second coming of Jesus very shortly. They do not, however, explicitly teach this, as we shall see in the following paragraph. Still, it is undeniable that such texts as 1 Th 5:1–5 and 2 Th 2:1–9 mirror the thoughts of a man who expects the Parousia immediately. Second Th also seems to be an entreaty to the people who had become indolent, since the end of time was "just around the corner" (cf. 2 Th 3:6–15). Not only Paul but the entire early Church as well considered the Parousia as imminent. This is shown by the following: "The end of all things is at hand" (1 Pet 4:7); "Little ones, the last epoch is here. You have heard that the antichrist is coming. Well, there are many antichrists now. By that fact we know that the last epoch is here" (1 Jn 2:18).

What is the New Testament teaching about the time of the Parousia? In a sentence: no one knew or knows, not even the Son of Man. It will come shortly, but who knows when? And this paradox is true. Both the imminence and the already more than 1900 years of delay are true. We are in the last age, the last days, and the last hours of the Messianic age, whose length has not been revealed and whose judgment is always too soon for those unprepared. The warnings of Mt 24 and 25, of Mk 13, and of Lk 21:8–36 are valid for an indefinitely short time!

b) *No one knows, not even the angels in heaven, nor yet the Son.* This translation almost manages to do away with a difficulty about the knowledge of Christ. If read carefully, it too allows us to see a certain lack in Jesus' knowledge, but the "nor yet" sounds a great deal like, "Well, it's just a little while and Jesus will know." The Greek text hardly permits such a toned-down version. The same negative is used for the angels and for Jesus! Mt is exactly faithful to Mk 13:32 in this instance, "No one knows, neither angels, nor the Son but only the Father."

The saying has all the hallmarks of being genuine, i.e., as having been spoken by Jesus. Some understand the saying to mean that Jesus has all the knowledge belonging to his mission; but since the knowledge of the Parousia was not necessary for his mission, he did not have it. Such an interpretation makes playacting of the humanity of Jesus. Jesus did not know "that day or hour" because, humanly speaking (and he was human), there was no way he could have known. We have discussed this experimental consciousness of Jesus under Mk 1:11 and Mk 14:32–42. We would add here only that Jesus must have said, on one occasion or more, that he did not know the time of the end of the world, the ultimate and definitive Day of the Lord. Mt and Mk saw no problem in a lack of knowledge in the Man and the king. Lk omits the saying.

2. In 24:37–42, Mt uses the Old Testament example of the flood, two parables, and a saying to teach that the Judge's coming

will be so unexpected that men will be doing their ordinary tasks when their fitness will be determined.

a) (24:37-39) *"As it was in the days of Noah, so it will be at the advent of the Son of Man in the days preceding the flood, people went on eating and drinking, marrying and giving in marriage, till the day when Noah entered the ark; and they suspected nothing till the flood came and swept them all away. So it will be at the advent of the Son of Man."*

The literary form, as mentioned, is an example story. Its teaching is that mankind went about its usual occupations at the time of Noah without being alert to God's coming. The same will happen before the Parousia.

It would not be right to conclude that Mt is teaching the historicity of the flood account. For him, the account is an example and he has passed no judgment on the flood as a thing that happened. Neither may we conclude that marriage is evil and should be avoided in these eschatological times, as some have concluded. Just as eating is not evil, so in these final times, marriage too is not evil. The teaching is that mankind will not be ready when the Man comes.

b) (24:40 f.) *"At that moment, if two are in the field, one may be taken up and one abandoned; if two women are grinding with the handmill, one may be taken up and one abandoned."*

The literary form of these two phrases is that of a parable, which gives one teaching through a fictitious story. Certainly, Mt is re-iterating his teaching that the Man will come suddenly, with no warning, i.e., when people are in the field and are grinding.

Is he also teaching that all should be prepared, for "two are working," but "one may be taken up and one abandoned?" We think this is true. Can we say, as many commentators do, that the "one who may be taken" is the one who is prepared; and, the "one abandoned" is the one who is condemned? If these parables were in a different context, or if we could see them as allegories, we would agree. We believe, however, that the example of Noah and the two parables are all dramatic ways of presenting the explicit sayings found in 24:42, "Keep awake; you do not know on what day your Lord returns;" and, in 24:36, "No one knows!" But we do not think that the argument is so strong in our favor that the student should not draw his own conclusion.

c) (24:42) *"Keep awake, therefore; you do not know on what day your Lord returns."* The literary form is a saying. The teaching is explicit: "Be on guard. He will come suddenly and without warning."

Who is "your Lord?" In this context, the term certainly refers to Jesus of Nazareth, and not God the Father. Does "Lord" have connotations? The Greek translation of the Bible, called the Septuagint, used *kyrios* to translate Yahweh. Paul certainly uses the term as a divine name, "There is a distribution of gifts, but the same Spirit (Third Person) distributes them. There is a distribution of ministrations, but it is the same Lord (*kyrios*; Second Person) to whom we minister. There is a distribution of activities, but it is the same God (First Person) who activates them all in everyone" (1 Cor 12:4-6). Luke also sometimes uses the term as a divine designation.

On the other hand, the term was used in the contemporary Hellenistic world as meaning "master, one in charge of a house, or people," and even as a title of rulers as "god." However, in the Synoptic Gospels, the term may mean no more than "sir," e.g., "Sir (*kyrie*), if you are willing, you can make me clean" (Mt 8:2).

In 24:42, moreover, we have a Matthean change of a text found in Mk 13:35 which reads, "Remain awake, therefore for you do not know when the *master of the house* returns." Is Mt using *kyrios* as synonymous with "master of the house?" Or is Mt steeped in the Old Testament's Septuagint translation, theologizing and saying "Keep awake; you do not know when your God returns." We prefer the first alternative, i.e., that Mt means no more than "your master, your King," but, choice is open.

Whichever is preferred, Jesus as God or as master, Mt's general teaching in 24:42 is clear: "Be prepared for the unexpected coming of Jesus."

Relating 24:36-42 to the entire Gospel of Mt. We have seen before that the king has come. He has inaugurated God's kingdom. Joy is the note of its members. Their goodness must be marked by the "law" of the Sermon. They will be judged, even though members of his kingdom, by a sudden and imminent second coming of the king. "Keep awake, for you know not when your punishing or rewarding king will come."

With these verses, we conclude our explanation of Mt's Gospel. His addition to the mosaic of Jesus is that of the king who revealed God's will and began God's kingdom. Response must be made. Would Christians carry on the murdering of the new prophets sent to them? Would they follow Jesus' law and love God?

CHAPTER THREE

Jesus in the Gospel According to Luke

Luke wrote both the third Gospel and the Acts of the Apostles (cf. below for proofs). Moreover, the third Gospel is the first part of at least two books, the second of which is the Acts. As Luke wrote, "In my former book, Theophilus, I spoke of all Jesus did and taught . . ." (Acts 1:1). Thus it is useful to introduce the author, importance, and summarize the teaching of both the third Gospel and Acts here.

Historical background. From the second half of the second century at the latest, the unanimous tradition of the early Church attributed the third Gospel to Luke. Irenaeus, the Muratorian Canon, Tertullian, Clement of Alexandria, Origen, and Jerome testified thereto.

Internal criticism pratically demonstrates the same. The author of the third Gospel and the author of the Acts of the Apostles is the same individual. Uniformity of each in vocabulary, style, form, and outlook indicates this. But the author of the Acts, as can be determined from the so-called "we-passages," could be only Luke. The minor of the above syllogism is proved from reading of the "we-passages" and by a process of eliminating all except Luke who could have been present when the "we-passages" were written.

The "we-passages" are Acts 16:10–17; 20:5–21:28; 27:1–28:16. Who was Luke? Luke was a highly educated Greek. He was also steeped in the knowledge of the Old Testament. He was Paul's companion. Tradition and Col 4:14 dub him a physician. A sixth-century tradition claims he was a painter who gave us the first picture of Mary. He was without doubt a literary artist, as we shall see in discussing his literary style. A psychologist has called Luke's temperament a combination of Francis of Assisi and Francis of Sales — a meek and joyful troubador of salvation. To see what the New Testament tells us about Luke, confer Col 4:14; Philem 23; 2 Tim 4:11, and the "we-passages" mentioned above.

Audience and date of the Gospel and the Acts. Luke addresses both books to a certain and otherwise unknown "Theophilus" (Lk 1:4; Acts 1:1). No matter what explanation is given concerning Theophilus, we can be certain that Luke had a wider audience in mind than a single individual. The audience envisioned for both books is that of Gentile Christians of a now unknown region. Scholars disagree about the dates of the two books. We prefer at the time of writing this book a date of A.D. 75 plus for the Gospel and around A.D. 80 plus for the Acts.

Importance of Luke. Luke's contribution to the mosaic of Jesus is especially that of the joyful Savior. More completely stated, Luke wishes to tell the joyful tidings that the Holy Spirit has brought the Savior of mankind. The Gospel describes how this Savior, after entering the Old Jerusalem, has, through his ministry, passion, and resurrection, delivered mankind (particularly the poor and sinful) from all distress and has himself entered the New Jerusalem of heaven. The Acts portray the Gospel's description as a type of what the spirit will do for the Savior-in-continuation (the Church).

Literary sources and style of Luke. Luke mentions his use of sources in his prologue, 1:1–4. It is safe to say that, of oral sources, certainly Luke interviewed Paul and other witnesses, including eye-witnesses. It may be that Mary was one whom he consulted. It seems probable that some other women influenced his Gospel.

Of written sources, we may conclude the following. Luke certainly used Mark's Gospel, improving Mark's style and adding his own elegance, but authorities disagree on the interrelation of Luke and Mt. Luke certainly, however, used written sources other than Mark (cf. p. ix).

Diverse styles are found in Luke which are usually exclusive to one of two ethnic groups, either the Hellenistic or the Semitic. The versatility of his style is apparent in no translation. If a Hebrew talks, the words and style employed by Luke are those of the Septuagint. If a Greek speaks, the classical, semi-classical, or Koine appropriate to the person is employed. These niceties are also untranslatable. But no translation can hide the picture stories that Luke presents: the good Samaritan, the Prodigal Son, the widow at Naim, the sinner in Simon's house, the "dwarf" Zaccheus, the repentant thief on the cross, the walk to Emmaus, etc.

OUTLINE OF LUKE'S GOSPEL

FIRST PART. Dawn of salvation (1:1–2:52; cf. 1:26–38).

SECOND PART. Investiture of Jesus (3:1–4:13).

  I. Preparation for the one who is to come (3:1–17).

  II. John's disappearance is Jesus' signal to appear as the Messiah and human Savior (3:18–4:13).

THIRD PART. The manifestation of the Savior in Galilee (4:14–9:50).

  I. Gentiles should not be surprised that the human Messiah, the Savior, was rejected by his own, after having been accepted by man. He had known that a prophet is never acceptable to his own. Too, this refusal was in God's designs to choose the Gentiles (4:14–30).

  II. Jesus — still having amazing teaching and power — chose Simon and others to save men (4:31–5:11).

  III. Jesus' new order (5:12–6:11).

  IV. The doctrines on charity which he, with his chosen Twelve, teaches to his disciples for all to hear, are destined to bring happiness to one who does them and woe to one who refuses to do them (6:12–49).

  V. Examples so that the Gentiles may know the different ways of responding to Jesus (7–8:21; cf. below 7:36–50).

  VI. The Gentiles should know that Jesus can save them no matter what the difficulty, if they have confidence in him (8:22–56).

VII. The humanly lowly Twelve have power and knowledge
from God. It was given to them as he prepared for the
crucifixion. These apostolic rights are above, but never
contrary to, that of other workers for Jesus (9:1–50).

FOURTH PART. The insistent preaching of salvation
(9:51–18:30).
   I. As salvation is being achieved, the chosen 72 publish it
as the merciful and joyful Good News. The needy can
believe that God became man. They too can merit the
life of the world to come by loving God (9:51–10:42).
  II. Luke teaches that prayer is persistent, confident asking
for the good spirit (11:1–13).
 III. Jesus cast out devils and raised men from the dead —
signs which brought some to follow him and led others
away (11:14–54).
 IV. Because of Jesus' passion, men must decide for or against
Jesus. Those who decide for him by expecting his coming
will be his divinely protected friends. Those who go
against him (even the leaders of the Church) will be
judged if they don't repent (12:1–59).
  V. The Jews, for the time being, have decided against
Jesus. Therefore their place is given to the Gentiles
(13:1–35).
 VI. His disciples: who can be his, what qualities they must
have, what advices they should remember (14:1–17:10;
cf. below 15:11–32).
VII. After once realizing that salvation is among them, the
Gentiles must prepare for its ultimate, sudden manifestation (the Parousia) by confident prayer, humility, keeping the commandments, and the right use of temporal
things. Thus, they will be rewarded now and hereafter
(17:11–18:31).

FIFTH PART. Jesus arrives at Jerusalem and dies there
(18:31–23:56).
   I. Introduction (18:31–19:28; cf. below 19:1–10).
  II. Yahweh-King-Messiah brings the sword of contradiction
to Jerusalem: heavenly peace to the disciples (the Gentiles and vengeful chastisement to the Jews (19:29–46).
 III. On the "eve of the passion" the leaders had rejected
God in Jesus' teachings — plotting to kill him, while
the generous poor honor God (19:47–21:4).
 IV. The prophecy of the ruin of the temple, and the great
eschatological warnings to all his disciples in view of the
destruction of Jerusalem and the Last Judgment (21:5–
36, 37 f.).
  V. The Passion (22:1–23:56).

    A. The Last Supper (22:1–38).

B. The Passion narrative proper (22:39–23:49).
C. The burial (23:50–56).
SIXTH PART: The resurrection and ascension (24:1–53).
I. The empty tomb is no place to look for the Living One, who had foretold his own resurrection. The disciples did not believe (24:1–12).
II. Emmaus. Faith shows that the Scriptures foretell his death and resurrection. Meeting him in his glory, through the Eucharist, causes an unforgettable experience (24:13–35).
III. Apparition of Jesus to the disciples. The risen Jesus is not a ghost. He should cause confidence, not fear (24:36–43).
IV. The ascension. Blessing God, they return overwhelmed with happiness (24:50–53).

Summary of Luke's teachings in the Gospel and Acts. Mark's plunge because of his anguished need for involvement in life cannot be found in Luke. Mt's safe guide to love is not nearly so detailed in the third Gospel as in the first. But then few of us live either constantly on the brink of life's involvement or in the staid and stolid sure steps of total love. Luke's serene joy, which is based on the fulfiller of salvation history and the gift of his spirit, is a more normal and liveable emotional mean.

Luke, the doctor, had experienced human misery. The converted Gentile heathen had known the vain nothingness of praying to gods. The educated and wealthy Christian missionary had seen the joy of a poor man's acceptance of Christ. Very naturally, therefore, did the fifty to sixty-year-old man concentrate on the Christian teachings of salvation, prayer, and joy.

The keynote of Luke's good news of salvation is joy — blessedness. "Blessed are you poor" (6:20; cf. 6:17–45). The notion of the peace of being blessed occurs again and again in Luke (cf. 10:23; 11:28; 12:37; 14:15). Luke tells his readers to be confident even in persecution and suffering (12:4–40). And Luke's nearly final verse in the Gospel tells how the disciples "in a transport of joy retraced their steps to Jerusalem" (24:52).

The news of salvation is joyful. For Luke, it was also prayerful. Jesus prays (6:12; 10:21 f.; 22:39–46). Persevere in prayer as a woman pestering a venal judge (18:1–8). Prayer must be humble, without the "I-trouble" of the Pharisee (18:9–14). It should be, "Father, may you be known and glorified . . ." (11:1–13).

Love — charity — is present in Luke's sermon, "Love your enemies; treat kindly those that hate you" (6:27; cf. 6:27–38). The example story of the good Samaritan teaches that any and all should be a recipient of kindness (10:25–37). And the delightful description of the visit of the Lord to Mary and Martha teach that the Lord must always be the one loved (10:38–42).

Joy, prayer, and love are taught by Luke. But most important is his message that redemption is here. His first two chapters depict salvation's dawn. Salvation from devils (4:33–44) and deliverance from death itself (8:40–56; 7:11–17) is at hand. Freedom for sinners has come (5:32; 7:36–50).

Three example-stories of the Lost Sheep, the Lost Coin, and the Lost Son are ageless proof of God's forgiving, solicitous love for man. His love for the sinner is so strong that it embraces the one out of the hundred who had strayed (15:1–7). God's longing for the sinner's conversion is like a woman who sweeps the house to find a lost coin — trifling in itself, but a treasure to her, and when found, a cause of delight to her (15:8–10). Most of all, his desire for a sinner's return is as generous, forgiving, embracing, anxious — loving — as a father toward a son who was lost. The father rushes to the son, interrupts his speech of contrition, clothes him as his son, and scolds the small-minded, scandalized, elder brother (15:11–32).

Salvation was proffered by God, but the Jews, despite miracles, had refused it (cf. 5:18–26; 6:6–11; 11:14–26; 19:11–28, etc.). Zaccheus (19:1–10) and the thief on the cross had accepted it, "I assure you, this very day you will be with me in paradise" (23:43).

Christ's redemptive act brought salvation. The Acts of the Apostles relates the expansion of the joyful news of man's deliverance from sin. The Lord had promised, "You shall be my witness in Jerusalem and in all Judea and Samaria and even to the very end of the earth" (Acts 1:8).

Almost every chapter of Acts teaches that in bringing about

salvation, God's power — God's spirit — is at work. Under the spirit, the word spreads from tiny Jerusalem (Acts 1:1–8:3) to the Samaritans (Acts 8:4–25), to all of Judea (Acts 8:40). Asia Minor and Europe soon have their communities of Christians (13:1–28:31).

Luke's heroes have their interesting tales of conquest. Peter told the fearsome Sanhedrin he was observing God's will (5:17–42). The Lystrans thought that Paul was a god (Acts 14:10). Philip converted the queen of Ethiopia's treasurer (Acts 8:26–40).

There were also times of trial and peril. Christ's stalwart emissaries were threatened with extinction. Peter was imprisoned (Acts 12); Stephen, martyred (Acts 6 and 7); James, killed (Acts 12:2); Paul tasted death, often (9:22–25; 12:50; 14:5–19; 19:23–40, etc.).

The budding Christ (the Church) was itself in the throes of conflict. A unity so perfect as that of Christ's Church (cf. Acts 2:42–46 and 3:32–37) had its Hellenistic and its Jewish factions nevertheless (cf. 6:1–11). Doctrine given by God seemed to contradict doctrine given by God. How were the early Christians to know which was right? Men asked, "Is circumcision necessary for salvation?" Peter stated the Christian dogma, "We believe that we are saved through the grace of our Lord Jesus!" (Acts 15:11).

Externally, the Church encountered opposition. The Greeks could not understand a resurrection (17:32). The Jews opposed this sect which accused them of deicide (2:36. ch. 21, etc.). The Romans were confused and as yet undecided (Acts 22–24).

And yet in all the tribulations told in the Acts, the teaching of joyful salvation is loudly proclaimed. For Christ conquers and is unconquerable. Who are his enemies? Gamaliel, Paul, death, shipwreck? They will succumb. Who must be won? Jews? By the thousands! Gentiles? By the nations and territories! Even in pagan Rome itself, Christ was invincibly unhindered — for how could Christ be enchained?

Salvation is here. It is ours. Luke depicts it. Only in Jesus is there salvation!

THE ANNUNCIATION. THE PROMISED SAVIOR, THE GREAT KING, THE HOLY, THE SON OF GOD WILL ENTER THE LIVING DWELLING OF GOD (1:26-38).

[26]In the course of the sixth month, the angel Gabriel came with a message from God to a town in Galilee called Nazareth. [27]He was to speak to a virgin espoused to a man named Joseph, a descendant of David. The name of the virgin was Mary. [28]On coming into her presence, he said, "Rejoice, child of grace! The Lord is your helper! You are blessed beyond all women!" [29]But she was profoundly disturbed by the address, and debated within herself what this greeting might mean. [30]So then the angel said to her: "Do not tremble, Mary! [31]You have found favor in the eyes of God. Behold: you are to be a mother, and to bear a son, and to call him Jesus! [32]He will be great: 'Son of the Most High' will be his title, and the Lord God will give to him the throne of his Father David. [33]He will be king over the house of Jacob forever, and to his kingship there will be no end!"

[34]Then Mary replied to the angel: "How will this be, since I remain a virgin?"

[35]In explanation the angel said to her: "The holy spirit will come upon you, and the power of the Most High will over-shadow you. For this reason, the child to be born will be ac-claimed 'Holy' and 'Son of God.' [36]Note, moreover: your rela-tive Elizabeth, in her old age, has also conceivel a son and is now in her sixth month — she who was called 'the barren'! [37]Nothing indeed is impossible with God." [38]Then Mary said: "Regard me as the humble servant of the Lord. May all that you have said be fulfilled in me!" With that, the angel left her.

General context and literary form. As in Mt Chapters 1 and 2, so in Lk 1 and 2, the literary form is that of midrash. This conclusion flows from the following considerations about the structure, teaching, and outline of Luke 1 and 2.

The literary structure of Luke 1 and 2. These first two chap-ters have a twofold structure: one static and one dynamic. Both arrangements are used to teach, as we shall see below.

1) The static structure can be seen from the artificial arrange-ment of events and from the refrains used:

    a) Artificial arrangements by scenes:

        1) Annunciation of John   2) Annunciation of Jesus
                3) Visitation
        4) Birth of John   5) Birth of Jesus

6) The Presentation/Purification
7) End of all six scenes: Jesus in the Temple
b) Refrains also help indicate an artificial structure:
1) Mary kept all these things in her heart
(cf. 2:19; 2:51);
2) The boy grew (cf. 1:80; 2:52).

2) The dynamic structure. Luke uses the Old Testament and/ or alludes to it in almost every verse of these two chapters. This is done to show the fulfillment of the Old Testament and to teach the dawn of the promised salvation. Some of the references are most evident; some, most allusive. But even the allusive would be evident to anyone who knew the Old Testament very well.

All groups have similar jargon. For example, "Private, the chaplain will punch your card," said to a rookie by his sergeant, would be diversely interpreted. Any soldier or veteran will know the ironical lack of sympathy in the sentence. The rookie's mother, happening by, might think that her boy had been given a real card which the chaplain was to punch, perhaps as a check on chapel attendance. Another example with which the reader of this book may be less familiar is, "he visits the spiritual director for his blanket." Any seminarian who is an avid reader of *Peanuts* would understand that the overdependence of a seminarian on his counselor is being described. An unlettered non-seminarian might think that some seminarians attended a class on the tricks of seances or spiritism.

In a similar way, someone not extremely familiar with the Old Testament would read Luke one and two and see only history and none of Luke's profound teaching. To introduce you to Luke's usage of the Old Testament we have grouped a few of the Old Testament allusions here and also shown some of the intricate reasoning behind one of the more evasive examples of Luke's use of the Old Testament:

a) Lk 1:26–36, cf. Zeph 3:14–17; Lk 1:23 f., cf. 2 Sam 7; Lk 1:35, cf. Ex 40:35; Lk 1:39–44, cf. 2 Sam 6:2–11; Lk 2:1–14, cf. Mic 4:7–5:5.

b) A more evasive example is Luke's reference to Daniel 8 and

9. Indications of this are:

1) "Gabriel" is used in all the Old Testament only in Dan 8:16 and 9:21, where the 70 weeks' "prophecy" is pronounced. In 9:21 Gabriel appeared at the hour of immolation.

2) Luke has Gabriel's name (1:26), has the hour of immolation (1:9), and has 70 weeks of 7 days. The 490 days arises from the following: 6 months (1:26) = 180 days + 9 months (period of pregnancy) = 270 days; + 40 days (presentation).

3) A confirmation that Luke willed the allusion to Dan 8 and 9: both Daniel and Luke take place in the Temple at the time of an offering (Lk 1:9) according to the prescription of the Law (1:9; 2:22,23,24,28). Also, Luke accentuates the "fulfilling" when a chronology is at issue (cf. 1:23 f.), the birth of Jesus (2:6) and presentation (2:22).

The literary form of these two chapters can thus be seen as midrashic, i.e. a drawing out of the Old Testament to teach a new, Christian reality. Luke, with a most complicated and artistic twofold structure, blends the Old Testament to the events to show the fulfillment. As said in our preface, this in no way either denies the statistical (historical) facts, or confirms them. Our commentary prescinds from such a query.

Summary of the influence of the structure and form on Luke's teaching in 1:4–2:52. Luke's narration of the infancy of Jesus of Nazareth teaches theology in a way different from that to which we are accustomed today. His method may be compared to the difference between a catechism's teaching and that of a Handel's *Messiah*. Both narrate historical truths, but Handel adds the vivaciousness of a skilled composer.

Luke uses the static events of the annunciations, births, visitation, purification, and the visit of Jesus to the Temple to teach. Each event also moves forward toward the greatest event: salvation in its day's dawn.

Luke has meditated upon the Old Testament to see its fulfillment in these events. The Child had a precursor, who was born in the most elaborate Old Testament conditions and was of a consecrated nature. The Child himself was Yahweh-Savior, the

Holy-Great, the Davidic King, the Light, the Glory. All of these titles and events lead to his first Word, "to be about the things of his Father" (2:49; my translation). The Messiah's first word was in the Temple and it was a choice of doing what his Father wanted. Salvation's dawn has arrived.

Outline of 1:1–2:52.

1:1–4   Prologue.
1:5–38 The promised Savior is announced — a Savior more perfect than the epitome of Old Testament perfection.
1:39–56 The living ark tends toward Jerusalem, praising God's fulfillment of his promises to the needy.
1:57–80 The marvel of the Precursor.
2:1–20 All, the lowliest and the most heavenly, marvel at the birth of the Messiah-Yahweh-Savior.
2:21–40 Yahweh-Savior's manifestation in the Temple. The beginning of Israel's being made clean.
2:41–52 The first word of Yahweh-Savior: his total dedication to the things of his Father. Salvation's dawn!

In the following pages, we shall explain Lk 1:26–38 in detail. We chose that pericope because it is a part of some chapters that are of great interest in these times. Moreover, we thereby have an opportunity of showing Luke's skill as a writer. We chose it chiefly, however, because the profound and timeless teachings of 1:26–38 about our Savior compelled us.

Summary of Lk 1:26–38. The Annunciation. The promised Savior, the Great, the King, the Holy, the Son of God will enter the living dwelling of God.

Exegesis of 1:26–38.

1. (1:26 f.). *In the course of the sixth month, the angel Gabriel came with a message from God to a town in Galilee called Nazareth. He was to speak to a virgin espoused to a man named Joseph, a descendant of David. The name of the virgin was Mary.* In sum, Luke teaches in these verses: In the sixth month, the heavenly messenger, Gabriel, was sent to an unknown village, to a virgin of the Davidic Joseph. The virgin's name was "Heavenly," or "Highest."

a) *In the sixth month:* this phrase was explained above (p. 90)

as being part of the fulfillment of the promise in Daniel. *Gabriel*:
the name "Gabriel" etymologically means "God is strong." As
we had mentioned under the literary form, Gabriel is the same
angel who appeared in Dan 8 and 9. Both of these chapters look
forward to the expected One. Therefore, Luke, in choosing
Gabriel, teaches the fulfillment of the Messianic times in the
messenger who is God's strength.

b) Nazareth is not mentioned in the Old Testament and thus
for Jews it was an unknown village. Reality began and ended with
the Bible and a village, if not biblically known, had no reality.
This mode of thinking is behind the teaching found in Heb 7:3;
Melchizedek "had no father, no mother, no genealogy. He had
neither beginning of days nor end of life." The Bible mentions
none of these particulars about Melchizedek and therefore they
did not exist. The same is true of Nazareth. Luke is drawing a
comparison between Jesus' annunciation — in obscurity — and
that of John in the most famous city of the Old Testament,
Jerusalem. He is beginning his teaching that the reality of the
New Testament exceeds Old Testament perfection.

c) The name "Mary" has received some sixty different etymolo-
gical explanations. In 1929, at Ras Shamra, in a language cognate
to Hebrew, Ugaritic, a text was found with the same name,
meaning "heavenly" or "most high." But, with at least 59 other
possibilities, to urge one would be rash.

The rest of the verse is easy. It repeats part of what we had
seen in Mt 1:18–25, but with stress on Mary. Joseph is of David's
house. Mary, his fiancee, is a virgin.

2. (1:28–31) *On coming into her presence, he said: "Rejoice,
child of grace! The Lord is your helper! You are blessed beyond all
women!" But she was profoundly disturbed by the address, and
debated within herself what this greeting might mean. So then
the angel said to her: "Do not tremble, Mary! You have found
favor in the eyes of God. Behold: you are to be a mother, and to
bear a son, and to call him Jesus!"*

In summary, these verses teach that the messenger told the one
full of God's favor (the Daughter of Zion) that joy should be

hers, not fear, because the Savior will dwell in her midst.

a) The translation, *rejoice*, sounds strange to us who are accustomed to saying the first words of the "*Hail, Mary.*" The Greek word translated *rejoice* can mean no more than the salutation, "Hail." However, we agree with the translation, "rejoice" because: (1) Lk 1 and 2 is midrashic; (2) the context is announcing the fulfillment of the Old Testament; and (3) because the word in the Old Testament in an emotional context always means *rejoice*. Luke is teaching the personified daughter of Zion (cf. below) that joy, messianic joy, should be hers.

b) *Child of grace* is Kleist's translation of the familiar "full of of grace." Either translation basically means the same. It is important to note that "grace" is not merely the theological sanctifying and actual grace. The term means one who is the object of God's love and thereby includes all the gifts of God. The participle used (*kecharitomene* — translation is "Child of grace" by Kleist) indicates by its tense and form that its possessor has the quality of God's favor in such a manner that it is overflowing. Note well, too, that Gabriel uses this title as the name of the one addressed. She is "the child of grace!" For a Semite, the name indicates the nature of the person. Thus, the Daughter of Zion (cf. next paragraph) is now the Child of grace. The title may refer to the office of the person, but the perfection and name indicate that the possessor of God's favor is equipped for the office.

Who is the child of grace? No one can deny the person named is Mary, in context. But because of Luke's midrashic use of Zeph 3:14–17 and Zach 9:9, Luke is teaching that Mary personifies the promised remnant, i.e., the Daughter of Zion. Compare the following quotation with these verses in Lk and see if the comparison is not too close to be coincidental, especially along with all the other Old Testament allusions in these chapters: "Shout for joy, O daughter of Zion! Sing joyfully, O Israel! Be glad and exult with all your heart, O daughter Jerusalem The Lord has removed the judgment against you, he has turned away your enemies; The King of Israel, the Lord is in your midst, you have no further misfortune to fear. On that day, it shall be said to Jerusalem:

Fear not, O Zion, be not discouraged! The Lord, your God, is in
your midst, a mighty Savior." (Hebrew: "Joshuah," same root as
"Jesus".)

We know that factually Mary, the person, was the epitome of
the poor and needy of the Old Testament. She personally em-
bodied all the good qualities God wanted in his people. She therefore was eminently fit to personify the Remnant, that group of
God's people who would be found loyal when the Promised One
came. She was uniquely apt to personify Zion's awaited daughter. And therefore, the Child of grace is the Daughter of Zion —
the recipient of God's gifts; this is Luke's teaching.

c) *The Lord is your helper* is the translation of the usual "The
Lord is with you." The phrase is used in the Old Testament exclusively, except for Ru 2:4, to mean the giving of a certain office
by God for the fulfilling of which God's presence as assured.
It is of note that God's aid is overcome, not to remove, difficulties. As a result, the one having the help was obliged to be
confident in God. The translation, therefore, "The Lord is your
helper" is excellent. The new Israel, the Daughter of Zion, will
have God's aid for its task; but, the new Israel must trust God.

d) *You are blessed beyond all women* is not genuine in this
verse. The words are missing in some of the best manuscripts.
Their absence is almost impossible to explain. Their presence is
explicable as an interpolation from 1:42 where they are genuine.

e) (1:31) *Behold: you are to be a mother, and to bear a son,
and to call him Jesus!* Kleist's translation "you are to be a
mother" obscures one of the Lucan indications of the midrashic,
literary form and also one of Luke's teachings on God's presence
to his new people. A slavishly literal translation runs, "You will
conceive in your womb." This redundant expression is intelligible
only if we look back to Zeph 3:14–17, quoted above. There, we
see that the "Lord is *in your midst.*" The artistic Luke could not
have been so brutish as to have added or left this detail of conception in the womb if it were not part of his teaching. Just as in
Zeph, so in Lk, Yahweh will be present to his people! How? Luke
will explain in the following verses.

f) With the explanations given already, the rest of the matter in these verses is easily understandable. The Daughter of Zion feared as the realization of the Messianic fulfillment deepened. How true this was of the early Church, the new Israel, Zion's Daughter! Trust and fear were and are the divine and human balances, as the Church weighs the frightening and delightful burden of who the Messiah is.

3. (1:32 f.) *He will be great: "Son of the Most High" will be his title, and the Lord God will give to him the throne of his father David. He will be king over the house of Jacob forever, and to his kingship there will be no end!* In summary, these verses teach that the Great One, who will be born, will be the Son of the Most High to whom the Lord God will give the throne of David, his Father, and of Jacob forever.

a) *He will be great.* The word "great" in the Old Testament, when used as an attribute and without further qualification, is limited to a divine designation. Luke used it here with this same meaning to describe the Child. This explanation is confirmed by the parallelism in titles given to John and Jesus. John is "great before God"; Jesus is "great." The early Church had the difficulty of describing Jesus as divine. Titles used of Yahweh were applied to Jesus, just as in present day theology when it "communicates idioms." In chapters one and two, not only "Great," but also "Light" and "Glory," formerly applied exclusively to Yahweh, are now attributed to Jesus.

b) *Son of the Most High* is, in this context, a divine title. It is true that in the Old Testament the title can refer to angels, kings, judges, and to the oppressed. Too, the New Testament indicates that Jesus was made Son in his resurrection (Rom 1:4; Acts 13:33). However, Lk 1:32 is assuredly using the title, "Son of the Most High," in a divine sense. Reasons for asserting this are: (1) This Gospel was written years after Jesus' resurrection, (2) it was written to Christians who believed him to be the Son of God, and (3) the context provides us with a convergence of divine titles. We are not trying to decide if this is statistical, i.e., if Mary knew her Son was God. We are saying that God's word is teaching that Jesus had a unique relationship with the Father, about which the word "Son" gives us some true but inadequate knowledge.

c) The rest of these verses is replete with Old Testament allusions. The expected Son of David of Is 9:5 f. and 2 Sam 7:12–16 has come. In sum, the Child in the care of the early Church was God's Son and the fulfillment of all the Old Testament promises regarding the one we call Christ.

4. (1:34) *Then Mary replied to the angel: "How will this be, since I remain a virgin?"* Did Mary make a vow or a promise of virginity? Did she do this before or after her engagement to Joseph? Did she intend to remain a virgin after the marriage? If the question in 1:34 is considered as an historical fact, these queries have place. If the question ever occurred, then we may ask our own questions about Mary's virginity. At the risk of incurring wrath both from those who are tired of hearing the assertion and also from those whose piety would be increased by discussing such questions, we reiterate that this commentary is not considering the "things that happened."

As a result, we are treating Luke's Gospel as God's inspired word and not deciding whether Mary ever asked Gabriel about her virginity. Mary, the personification of the new Israel, admits her need, her lack. In other words, the "poor in spirit" tells God's messenger that the New Israel is needy. The teaching is extremely profound. The early Church's initial response to its God is to admit its need — in this impossible circumstance!

Moreover, because of the parallel with the incident in John's annunciation when Zachary was punished for asking the question, (cf. 1:18 f.), we may conclude that the New Israel had the right, in all faith and trust, to question God, as did many psalms and the book of Job.

In summary, then, Luke teaches in 1:34 that the Daughter of Zion is in need, is lacking, and has the right to question.

5. (1:35) *In explanation, the angel said to her: "The holy spirit will come upon you, and the power of the Most High will overshadow you. For this reason the child to be born will be acclaimed 'Holy' and 'Son of God.' "*

a) *The holy spirit* means God's power for some particular task. Even in this context there is little reason for urging a meaning of the Third Person, for the same reasons we have seen in Mk 1:10. Moreover, the parallelism between "the holy spirit" and "the power of the Most High" require that the spirit mean the same as God's power. The teaching is that the lack even in this impossible situation will be filled up by God.

b) *The power of the Most High will overshadow you.* The Greek word Luke uses for "overshadow" is *episkiadzei*. The usual word in the Septuagint for Yahweh's spirit's coming over someone is different. *Episkiadzō* occurs only three times in the Old Testament. (Cf. Pss 90 [91]: 4; 139 [140]: 8; Ex 40:35.) Etymologically, *episkiadzein* means "to shadow over." The Septuagint chose it to express God's cloud's overshadowing, i.e., the Shekinah's protection!

With this background, we think it will be easy to understand the Lukan midrashic use of Ex 40:35, "The cloud settled down upon it and the glory of the Lord filled the dwelling." In such a way, Luke teaches that Mary is the personification not only of the Daughter of Zion, but also of the Ark of the Covenant. God's power, God's Shekinah, will symbolize God's effective presence, just as it did in the Old Testament. And just as God dwelt in the Ark, so now he will dwell in the Daughter of Zion, the Ark.

c) *For this reason the child to be born will be acclaimed "Holy" and "Son of God."* "Will be acclaimed" is a Semitic way of expressing "will be." The translation of the rest of this phrase is difficult. Whatever translation be preferred, the meaning will come out that the child will be "Holy" and "God's Son." It is of note that the word for "holy" is neuter, not masculine. He will be more than human. The verse is pregnant with meaning. What does "holy" mean? What does it mean to have a unique relationship to God which is titled "Son?" Both concepts are worthy of the student's meditation, just as the Church some 2,000 years later continues meditating on the "Holy Son of God."

d) In summary, then, 1:35 teaches that the action of God's

spirit and the divine Shekinah shall cause to be born, from the
Ark, the Holy, the Son of God.

6. (1:36 f.) *Note, moreover: your relative Elizabeth, in her
old age, has also conceived a son and is now in her sixth month
— she who was called "the barren"! Nothing indeed is impossible
with God.* Abraham's wife, Sarah, was barren until very old. The
early Church knew that all things were possible to God. But
could it act with trust, even in the impossible? God had given
proofs in abundance. Luke here refers to Elizabeth's conception
out of due time as an example of what God can do. Will the
Daughter of Zion, the new Ark, trust in God to do even the
impossible?

7. (1:38) *Then Mary said: "Regard me as the humble servant
of the Lord, May all that you have said be fulfilled in me!" With
that, the angel left her.* The Daughter of Zion's willingness to
trust God starts the fulfillment of the promise in Gen 3:15, made
after the mother of mankind had shown her unwillingness.

Relating 1:26–38 to the entire Gospel of Luke. Luke teaches
that the Annunciation of the promised one has come about. He
is the Savior, the Great, the King, the Holy, the Son of God.
He will dwell in God's Ark, the Daughter of Zion. Luke's Gospel
continues to unfold the Savior's salvation. Luke will also teach
the joy and prayer which are the needed response of a lacking
Daughter, the early Church.

THE SINNER AND THE "SINLESS"
(Lk 7:36–50).

[36]One day, one of the Pharisees invited him to a meal with
him. He entered the home of the Pharisee and reclined on a
couch; [37]and without warning a woman who was a scandal in the
town came in. After making sure that he was at table in the home
of the Pharisee, she brought with her an alabaster flask of perfume, took her stand behind him at his feet, and wept. [38]Yielding
to an impulse, she rained her tears on his feet and wiped them
with her hair; she tenderly kissed his feet and anointed them
with perfume. [39]His host, the Pharisee, noticed this and said to
himself: "This man, if he were a prophet, would know who and
what sort of creature this woman is, that makes so much fuss
over him! Why she is a scandalous person!"

⁴⁰Jesus read his thoughts and said to him: "Simon, I have something to tell you." "Tell it, Rabbi," he replied. ⁴¹"Once upon a time two men were in the debt of a money lender. The one owed him five hundred denarii; the other fifty. ⁴²Neither of them was in a position to pay; so he made both of them happy by canceling their debts. Under the circumstances, which of them will be more generous in loving him?" ⁴³"The one, I suppose," answered Simon, "whom he made happy by canceling the greater amount." "Your judgment is correct," he replied. ⁴⁴Then, turning to the woman, he said to Simon: "Do you see this woman? I came into your house, and you offered me no water for my feet: but this woman rained her tears upon my feet and wiped them dry with her hair. ⁴⁵You gave me no kiss of welcome; but this woman has not left off, from the time I entered, tenderly kissing my feet. ⁴⁶You did not anoint my head with oil: but this woman anointed my feet with perfume. ⁴⁷And in consideration of this I tell you; her sins, numerous as they are, are forgiven. You see, she has shown much love! One, of course, who has but little forgiven him, shows but little love." ⁴⁸He then said to her: "Your sins are forgiven." ⁴⁹At once his fellow guests gave way to thoughts like this: "Who is this individual who even forgives sins!" ⁵⁰He finally said to the woman: "Your faith has saved you. Go home and be at peace."

General context. Lk 7:36–50 falls within the Gospel's third general part, namely: The Savior's manifestation in Galilee (4:14–9:50). From 7:1–8:21, Luke gives examples so that the Gentiles may know the different ways one can respond to Jesus. The centurion, the widow of Naim, John the Baptist, the publicans and Pharisees, the sinful woman and "sinless" Simon, many women — all respond to the Savior. Finally Luke tells of hearing his words.

We have chosen this section because it beautifully and profoundly shows Luke's teaching about sin and salvation.

Literary form. A story about Jesus, containing a strict parable. Therefore, Luke will be teaching one and only one point, namely: "One, of course, who has but little forgiven him shows but little love."

Exegesis of Lk 7:36–50.

1. (7:36–38) Setting of the scene. A Pharisee's banquet at which a woman sinner shows superabundant marks of hospitality

to the Master. The hospitality of a Jew to his guest was taken
for granted. It was to be shown in giving water to wash the
feet, a formal welcoming in the form of a kiss of peace, and at
least a little oil against the scorchingly hot sun. Hospitality was
and is one of the chief virtues of the Semitic peoples. Its lack
was a sign of an insult.

2. (7:39) The occasion of the parable. The Pharisee doubted
that Jesus was God's spokesman, a prophet. The reason for his
doubt was that Jesus was not cautious in allowing people to
minister to him.

3. (7:40–50) The parabolic teaching:

a) (7:40–43) The puzzle of the parable was easily solved by
Simon. In fact, read carefully, there is scorn in the pithy minored
key of "The one, I suppose, whom he had made happy by
cancelling the greater amount."

b) (7:44–48) The Parable's application is given a different
twist by Jesus. As a result, as we shall see, the parable is not
quite applicable to the woman, but is pointed at Simon.

Simon had answered the parable in its most evident sense. One
forgiven 500 denarii will in all probability be more grateful than
someone forgiven 50. But Jesus twists the parable to "One, of
course, who has but little forgiven him shows but little love."
Jesus' solution of the parable turns his previous question from
one who loves more to one who loves less! And Simon has been
caught! The parable then becomes applicable to the "sinless" and
"just" Pharisee!

Luke's teaching, it goes without saying, is both psychologically
and theologically sound. Psychologically, people generally proceed
from sin to repentance, to thanksgiving for forgiveness, and then
to love. As a result, psychologically, the one "to whom little is
forgiven, loves little."

Theologically, too, no one loves who is not redeemed. As Lk
says, "He to whom little is forgiven, loves little." Father Liege
in *What is Christian Life?* has rightly said, "The citizen knows
what it is to break the rules, the good man understands the meaning of wrong, the saint knows sin. . . . In the life of the saint

there is no room for the Pharisee." To the extent that a man understands sin and his sinfulness he loves gratefully the good, forgiving God more. As Paul wrote near the end of his life, "Trustworthy and deserving of wholehearted acceptance is the saying, 'Christ Jesus came into the world to save sinners.' Of these I am at the head of the list" (1 Tim 1:15). Luke himself has again written the same truth in, "Apply this to yourselves: when you have carried out all the orders given you, just say: 'We are good-for-nothing slaves; we have merely done our duty' " (17:10).

c) (7:49 f.) This and the following verse teach that Jesus' claim to forgive sins makes many marvel. He sends the sinful woman away in total happiness — saved by her confidence in him.

Relating 7:36–50 to Luke's entire Gospel. The Savior has brought salvation. The salvation is from sin. The self-made saint, i.e., the one who relies on himself to be holy, prevents God. Trust in God and that God will forgive even a great sinner like me, can make me holy, can overcome the fear that results in self-reliance. For Luke, holiness is a personal encountering of the nothingness of each individual with the Savior. It is the total emptying of self to admitting, "I am a sinner." It results in the joy and happiness that holiness causes — the nothingness of self to be made into the fulness of God's gift. "One, of course, who has but little forgiven him, shows but little love" (7:47). But also, "Go home and be at peace" (7:50).

THE LOST-FOUND AND EGOTISTICAL SONS
(Lk 15:11–32).

[11]"Once upon a time," he said, "a man had two sons. [12]One day the younger of them said to his father: 'Father, give me the part of property that falls to my share.' So he divided his property between them. [13]Not many days later, the younger son cashed everything and went off to a far-off country, where he squandered his money by licentious living. [14]When he had spent everything, a terrible famine swept over that country and he faced starvation. [15]So he went to throw himself on the mercy of a citizen of that region, who sent him to his farm to tend pigs. [16]And oh, how heartily he would have feasted on the pods on which the pigs were feeding! But no one would give them to him. [17]At last he

came to his senses. 'How many of my father's hired men,' he said, 'have food enough and to spare, while I am perishing with hunger. [18]I will quit this place and go to meet my father. Father, I will say to him, I have sinned against heaven, and you know [19]that I am no longer fit to be considered your son. Treat me as one of your hired help.' [20]So he quit the place and went to meet his father.

"He was still a good way off when his father caught sight of him and, stirred to pity, ran and threw his arms round his neck and kissed him affectionately.

[21]"The son then said to him: 'Father, I have sinned against heaven and before you, and you know that I am no longer fit to be considered your son.' [22]But the father said to the slaves: 'Quick! bring out the finest robe and put it on him; then put a ring on his hand and sandals on his feet; [23]also fetch the fatted calf and kill it; let us feast and celebrate. [24]This son of mine was dead and has come back to life again, was lost and has been found again.' And so they gave themselves up to celebrating.

[25]"Meanwhile, the elder son was in the field. When he returned and came near the house, he heard strains of music and dancing, and [26]calling one of the farmhands aside, inquired what all this meant. [27]'Why,' the lad said to him, 'your brother has come back; so your father had the fatted calf killed because he received him back safe and sound.' [28]Thereupon he grew angry and refused to go in. So his father came out and pleaded with him. [29]But he protested and said to the father: 'Look at all these years that I have been toiling like a slave for you! I have never disobeyed any of your orders, and yet you never gave me a kid, that I might celebrate with any friends! [30]But here comes that son of yours who wasted his property in the company of lewd women, and right away you kill the fatted calf to humor him!' [31]He replied: 'My son, you have always been with me, and all that is mine is yours; [32]but as to this feasting and celebrating — it simply has to be done, because that brother of yours was dead and has come to life again, was lost and has been found again!' "

General context. Chapter 15:11–32 falls within the fourth part of St. Luke's Gospel, the insistent preaching of salvation (9:51–18:30). From 14:1–17:10 Luke exemplifies the qualities which a disciple of Christ should, and should not, have. Christians must have a proper attitude toward the Sabbath, toward self-sufficiency, toward selfish giving, and toward confidence based on nationality (cf. 14:1–24). One of the positive qualities which a disciple must have is a calculated renunciation of all obstacles, lest disaster be courted, 14:25–36. Finally, in 15:1–32, Luke teaches that the just should not be scandalized if sinners are welcomed by the God who rejoices in seeking them out.

We have chosen 15:11–32 not only because of its unsurpassed literary beauty but also because of its picture of God's love for us sinners. It has been rightly called the gospel of Luke's Gospel. It capsulizes his good news of joyous salvation, "Glory to God and peace on earth!" (cf. Lk 2:14).

Literary form. An allegorical parable. While there is one special teaching to this parable, there are some allegorical elements. We shall indicate these in the exegesis.

Exegesis of 15:11–32.

1. (15:11–13) The Jewish law gave one third of the property to the youngest son on the death of the father (cf. Dt 21:15–17). Although the advance in this case was given before the death of the father, there are some other similar biblical examples (cf. Tob 8:21; Sir 33:24). Needless to say, the son had no right to the advance.

Later we shall point out that the father is allegorically to be interpreted as God. Whether the allegory has already begun, so that God allows the son to go into temptation or not, is up to the student to decide. 15:11–13 may be only an introduction to the story. The younger son is a sinner.

2. (15:14–16) After the son had thrown away his share of the inheritance on loose living, "he went to throw himself on the mercy of a citizen of that region, who sent him to his farm to tend pigs. And oh, how heartily he would have feasted on the pods on which the pigs were feeding!"

Luke's artistry is admitted by all. A fortune went down the drain. A famine caused the entire region to want. This young Jew, starving, was sent to care for the unclean animal called a pig. So hungry was he that he would eat the insipid and hardly-fit-for-human-consumption pods of the carob tree!

3. (15:17–20) Hoping for the same food and treatment as one

of his father's slaves, the son starts his journey for home. *He was still a good way off when his father caught sight of him, and, stirred to pity, ran and threw his arms round his neck and kissed him affectionately.*

The picture presented is that of a man in constant vigil for the return of his son. He runs out to meet his son. The father is so overwhelmed with joy that he cannot speak. There is no scolding, no hesitation. Rather, joy and eagerness for the reunion predominate.

4. (15:21) Before, in 15:18b–20, the son had memorized the apology which he considered necessary to give. He would say, "I have sinned against heaven, and you know that I am no longer fit to be considered your son. Treat me as one of your hired help." The father never let him finish. When the son got as far as, "You know that I am no longer fit to be considered your son. . . ," the father interrupted.

5. (15:22 f.) No apology! No reprimand! Neither made a slave nor an outcast! The father imposes on his son the signs of a free man. A ring and sandals were signs that a man was free. The son's return was a time of unlimited joy, "the fatted calf."

6. (15:24) *"This son of mine was dead and has come back to life again, was lost and has been found again." And so they gave themselves up to celebrating.* Although this parable has been called the "Prodigal Son," this is a misnomer. The point of the parable is the "Found" Son. It would be much better named, "The Lost and Found Son." Thus too, it would match the two parables preceding, the "Lost and Found Sheep" (15:1–7), and the "Lost and Found Coin" (15:8–10). Whatever its name, the allegorical point of this son is evident: he is the repentant son of God, the father!

7. (15:25–32) Luke's picture of the pouting, jealous, and petulant elder son is as artistic as the preceding one of the father and the younger son. Outside, the elder son inquires from the servants what is going on in his own house. On learning the cause, he became angry, even after the evidently joyous attitude of the servant. Even though the father begged, the elder had to

lecture his father on his own goodness and his brother's evil. "What kind of father are you who would humor this type of son and not appreciate the excellent son you have?" And, of course, this type of father cannot understand such an outlook: *"My son, you have always been with me, and all that is mine is yours; but as to this feasting and celebrating — it simply has to be done, because that brother of yours was dead and has come to life again, was lost and has been found again!"* It simply has to be done!

Who is the elder brother? What allegorical point does he bring forth? Although Luke addressed this chapter to the Pharisees and Scribes (cf. 15:2) we believe that he does not allegorize the elder son as a picture of the evil Pharisees. These Pharisees are never pictured in the New Testament as merely pettily self-centered, as is the elder son. Gravely selfish and insincere would be their proper New Testament designations. Moreover, the admonition of 15:31 f. would not fit a Pharisee. He was no longer God's son, as a Christian would have understood. By A.D. 75 it could no longer be said of him that "all that is mine is yours."

Therefore, we conclude that the elder son is any normally "good" person. Having kept God's laws, he easily forgets how much he needs God. Too easily does he forget that he too has been redeemed. All that God has is his son's — but as a gift. As Paul put it, "Where, then, is any reason for boasting? It is excluded" (Rom 3:27).

Relating 15:11–32 to Luke's entire Gospel. Luke's Gospel is the good news of salvation. In this picture, he answers queries about salvation, "Why should God be concerned about the sinner? Why chase after him? Why welcome him back? Why become contaminated by "personal" contact? Luke's answer is simply, "God loves a sinner, each individual sinner that much!" Luke's Gospel is summarized in the "Lost–Found Son and the Egotistical Son." It speaks louder than any words of ours could concerning its relation to Luke's entire good news of the joy of salvation.

PRUDENT DEDICATION TO HOLINESS ESPECIALLY IN REGARD TO TEMPORAL GOODS (Lk 16:1–13).

¹He also said to the disciples: "Once upon a time, there was a rich man who had a manager, and complaints were made to him about this man that he was letting his estate go to rack and ruin. ²So he summoned him and said: 'What is this I hear about you? ³Submit your balance sheet! You can be manager no longer!' The manager then reasoned as follows: My master is taking the management away from me. What shall I do? To dig I am not strong enough; to beg I am ashamed. ⁴Ah, I know what to do, so that, when I am ousted from the management, people will welcome me in their homes!' ⁵And calling his master's debtors to appear before him, one by one, he said to the first: 'How much do you owe my master?' ⁶One hundred barrels of oil,' he replied. 'Take your note,' he said to him: 'quick, sit down and write fifty.' ⁷'And you,' he said to another, 'how much do you owe?' 'Fourteen hundred bushels of wheat,' he replied. 'Take your note,' he said to him, 'and write eleven hundred.' ⁸And the master commended the unscrupulous manager for his shrewd way of acting.

The fact is, in dealing with their own kind, the children of the world are shrewder than the children of the light. ⁹And so I say to you: money is a worthless thing; but use it to make friends for yourselves, so that, when it gives out, they may receive you in the everlasting homes. ¹⁰He who is conscientious in small things is conscientious in big things also. ¹¹Therefore, if you do not prove conscientious in handling so worthless a thing as money, who will trust you with a genuine good? ¹²And if you do not prove conscientious in handling what is not your own, who will trust you with what is your own?

¹³A servant cannot be the slave of two masters; for either he will hate the one and love the other, or, at least, be attentive to the one and neglectful of the other. You cannot have God and money for masters!"

General context. Chapter 16:1–13 continues the general context of a disciple's qualities which we summarized in the introduction to 15:11–32 on p. 102. These verses teach that since God and the world are incompatible, temporal things must be used in relation to God. We shall see 16:1–13 in detail later. Money is not a sign of God's blessing to the individual is the theme of 16:14–31. The right understanding of the Old Testament proves this. A right understanding of the kingdom of God proves the same. Lastly, an example of the future life proves this thesis.

Literary form of 16:1–13. Chapter 16:1–8 is a parable with a few allegorical elements, and 16:9–13 contains sayings.

We chose these verses because they are somewhat difficult and because, in brief form, they show the completely dedicated devotion that Luke requires of a Christian toward temporalities.

Exegesis of 16:1–13.

1. (16:1–8) This is a parable which teaches that one should dedicate himself to holiness, with all the shrewdness of a desperate man. Most of the parable is easily understandable once its background is known.

a) (16:1 f.) The manager is presented as already guilty. It does not follow that the conduct narrated in 16:3–7 is wrong.

b) (16:3–7) Palestinian laws allowed a commission to the manager when he collected debts. The manager of this story called in his master's debtors and refused his considerable commission. He thereby hoped to gain the good-will of many people, 16:4.

c) (16:8a) His master commends his shrewd way of acting, i.e., giving up his commission to gain good will.

d) In 16:8b, the point of the parable is laid down in no uncertain language. *The fact is, in dealing with their own kind, the children of the world are shrewder than the children of the light.* "The children of . . ." is a Semitism for the "nature of" plus whatever follows. In this case, the children are sinners, for "world" is here being used in a pejorative sense, as the context requires. The term "children of light" is found in the "Qumran" scrolls and Paul (1 Th 5:5) to mean "the chosen."

The point of the parable is that Christians can learn from the "sharpies" of this world to act prudently and dedicatedly in the crisis of Christianity. How often have you heard it said about a bank robber, "if he had put his talents and energy to good, he would have been successful!" For "the children of the world are shrewder than the children of the light!"

2. In 16:9–13, Luke applies this general principle of prudence and dedication by giving sayings on using temporal goods for the ultimate end. These verses are troublesome. We will lay down (A) the problems; (B) the certainty; (C) a key to solving the problems; (D) a general statement of the verses' figures; (E) application of the key to the particular texts.

A) The problems: In 16:9b, what is meant by "they may receive you into everlasting homes?" In 16:10, what are "small and big things?" In 16:11, what are "genuine and worthless things?" In 16:12, what are "your own and not your own things?"

B) The certainty is found in 16:13. "You cannot have God and money for masters." The Greek word for Kleist's translation "money" is Mammon. In parallel with God, there is, we think, an obvious personification of Mammon, just as in Mt 6:24.

C) A key to solving the problems: Luke is personifying throughout these verses. Proofs that he is so doing are the "friends" and "welcoming into everlasting homes (*skēnas*)" of 16:9; and "others and your own" of 16:12. We would conjecture that the "Unjust Mammon" (Kleist's translation: "worthless money") of 16:11 is a personification, paralleled by "The Genuine" (Kleist's translation: "genuine good").

D) General statement of the personification. In Master God's kingdom (16:13), the child of light (16:8b) is destined for an everlasting home, where he will find the big and the genuine, and his own things. But the perplexity of this child of light is that he now exists in master mammon's kingdom. In master mammon's kingdom are things worthless, small, and foreign to a child of light. The child of light must therefore make "friends" with master mammon's things to "buy" his way into his rightful and everlasting home.

E) Application of the figures to the sayings of 16:9–13:

a) (16:9) Instead of Kleist's translation, we would prefer, and this is in keeping with the Greek, "Make friends (i.e., join the group of) the Unjust Mammon, so that when it fails, you may be received (a third person plural used semitically for a passive) into the everlasting homes." This saying teaches a Christian to know how to use all temporal goods for their own proper end (i.e., temporal) so that God may welcome him into God's dwelling.

b) (16:10) *He who is conscientious in small things is conscientious in big things also.* The small things are the temporal and comparatively unimportant.

c) (16:11) Instead of Kleist's, we prefer, "If therefore you are not conscientious in Unjust Mammon, who will trust you in The Genuine?" If, in other words, a Christian fails in his use of unimportant things, those belonging to Unjust Mammon, how can God reward him with the big and genuine?

d) (16:12) *And if you do not prove conscientious in handling what is not your own (i.e., that of Unjust Mammon's), who will trust you with what is your own (i.e., that of God's, of the Light's)?*

Relating 16:1–13 to Luke's entire Gospel. The sayings in 16:9–13 are difficult. Perhaps just for that reason you will remember them more easily. We think that Luke's meaning is as clear as it is difficult for us today to follow. "Use this world's goods to enter God's house," he says.

Salvation has come in the Savior. His love for the sinner has been taught. How respond? A child of light must live as shrewdly as a child of the world. He must indeed make "friends" with mammon, just as a manager who relinquishes his worldly goods, those belonging to the people of the world, the insignificant, so that he too will be welcome in people's homes. Prudence and dedication in the crisis of Christianity are difficult. But it is impossible to serve both Master God and Master Mammon.

SALVATION TO A RICH AND REPENTANT SINNER (Lk 19:1–10).

[1]He now entered Jericho. As he made his way through the town, [2]there was a stir: a man named Zaccheus, a high official among the tax collectors and rich as well, [3]was curious to find out who Jesus was, but owing to the press of people, had no chance to do so, for he was small of stature. [4]In order therefore, to get a glimpse of Jesus, he ran ahead and climbed up into a sycamore tree, because he was expected to pass that way. [5]When Jesus

came to the spot, he looked up. "Zaccheus," he said to him, "come down quickly; today I must be your guest." ⁶And, coming down quickly, he welcomed him joyfully. ⁷But a murmur ran through the crowd of spectators. "He has turned in," they commented, "to accept the hospitality of a sinner!" ⁸Then Zaccheus drew himself up and addressed the Lord: "Upon my word, Lord, I will give to the poor one half of my possessions and, if I have obtained anything from anybody by extortion, I will refund four times as much." ⁹Then in his presence, Jesus said: "Today salvation has visited this household, because he, too, is a son of Abraham. ¹⁰After all, it is the mission of the Son of Man to seek and save what is lost."

General Context. Lk 19:1–10 falls within the fifth Part of Luke's Gospel, Jesus Arrives at Jerusalem and Dies there (cf. 18:31–23:56). The introduction to the Passion narrative extends from 18:31–19:28. In 18:31–34, Luke teaches how difficult the Twelve found it to understand the passion and death of the Messiah. In 18:35–43, Luke teaches that faith to follow Yahweh-Savior to suffering and ultimate victory will be given if perseveringly asked. In 19:1–10, as we shall see, salvation is given. Lk 19:11–28 teaches Jesus' ultimate triumph which will bring victory or chastisement.

Literary form of 19:1–10. This is an example-story. An example-story may be classified as a type of a parable in which a person or persons are used to bring out a teaching. The Good Samaritan is also an example-story.

We have chosen this pericope because of its literary beauty, and, more especially, because of its teaching that even a rich sinner can be saved.

Exegesis of 19:1–10.

1. (19:1–4) A rich publican in charge of a wealthy district wanted to see Jesus but was too small to succeed. He therefore climbed a tree to see him. The picture is quickly and beautifully painted.

It helps to know that the term "tax collector," i.e., a publican, was practically synonymous with sinner. The reason was that in those days a tax collector was assigned a certain region to collect a determined amount. Everything over and above the amount required by Rome was his own. As a result, many tax collectors imposed extremely high taxes. Zaccheus must have been in a prosperous area, since he had become rich from the area. Luke's teaching will be concerning a sinner, and a rich one at that.

Luke is not teaching that curiosity and the embarrassment of climbing a tree are dispositions for salvation. Zaccheus' interest and tree climbing are part of his picture, not of his teaching. The rich man wanted to see Jesus. He wanted to see him so badly that he was willing to display his lack of height, so the picture goes.

2. (19:5) *When Jesus came to the spot he looked up. "Zaccheus" he said to him, "come down quickly; today I must be your guest."* The picture needs no explanation, except for the technical term "I must" which Luke uses.

The term translated "I must" is *dei* in the Greek. Literally, *dei* means "It is necessary." The New Testament generally used it as a term meaning "divinely predestined." It is used especially about the passion of Christ. Christ's passion "was necessary," i.e., God had predestined the Messiah, Christ, to suffer and die. Luke uses *dei* in his Gospel and Acts forty-four times. God had willed Jesus' discussion with the doctors in 2:49; his preaching throughout city after city in 4:43. God had willed Jerusalem's fall (cf. 21:9). So here, in 19:5, God had willed that salvation come to Zaccheus. Luke has begun his teaching and stepped out of merely picturizing.

3. (19:6 f.) *With joy, hastening, Zaccheus welcomes Jesus.* But, the people judge, *"He has turned in to accept the hospitality of a sinner!"*

4. (19:8) *Then Zaccheus drew himself up and addressed the Lord: "Upon my word, Lord, I will give to the poor one half of my possessions, and, if I have obtained anything from anybody by extortion, I will refund four times as much."* The little man draws himself up! His generosity is great. Rabbinical law required a thief to restore fourfold. Zaccheus does this and adds one half of his possessions. Luke uses a mood (the indicative)

and tense (the aorist) which leaves no doubt as to Zaccheus' being a sinner. Zaccheus says, "If I have obtained anything from anybody by extortion, as I really have. . . ."

5. (19:9 f.) *Then, in his presence, Jesus said: "Today salvation has visited this household, because he, too, is a son of Abraham. After all, it is the mission of the Son of Man to seek and save what is lost."*

Zaccheus' reward! Zaccheus' entire household receives the salvation promised to a genuine son of Abraham. The Messiah had come to look for and save sinners. Every Gentile reading Luke's Gospel would know that he too could hope in salvation. Luke did not mention whether Zaccheus was an Israelite or not. The important teaching is that Christianity is not ethnically delimited. The Savior has come to redeem all sinners.

19:1–10 is an excellent summary of Luke's Gospel. The Savior has come. He seeks the lost. Salvation can enter a sinner's house. Not only in direct teaching, but also in memorable pictures has Luke contributed joyous salvation to the mosaic of the Synoptic's Jesus. The Savior saves. The joy found in living Christianity and personally encountering the Savior can be anyone's!

Epilogue

To explain the Gospels is a challenge. To accept the challenge is to play the fool. To be the object of the fool is frustrating for the reader. Frustration should be lessened slightly if the reader has achieved a frame of mind of asking, when he next hears or reads the Gospels, "What does Mk mean to teach his Roman Christians about the year A.D. 65 by 'these' verses? What does Mt teach his Hebrew Christians around A.D. 75 by 'these' verses? What does Luke wish to teach his Gentile Christians around A.D. 80 by 'these' verses? What does each evangelist add to the mosaic who is Christ?" If the reader asks those questions and not "What did Jesus do or mean by this?" his studies will have been richly rewarding.

Ten years ago, the author of this book began a life of Christ to be entitled, *The Man of Sorrows*. It was never finished, and it could not be. After teaching the Gospels and after finishing JESUS IN THE SYNOPTIC GOSPELS, the author's fundamental approach to Jesus — the failure of Mark, the King of Matthew, and the joyful Savior of Luke — is to a personality so compelling, so charming, and so happy that he simply was not "The Man of Sorrows."

Little children could not have approached a begruntled failure. An aloof monarch could not have proclaimed, "Oh the happinesses of the poor." Only a man who saw that he was somehow affecting mankind in his own drudgery, his own walking the streets of Nazareth could have brought the joy which Luke paints.

With these pages, the book is completed. As said, to explain the Gospels is a challenge which only a fool would accept. May the One portrayed in the Gospel accounts of Mark, Matthew, Luke, fill up with his humanity, kingship, and joyful salvation, the lack and need of the fool who composed this text.

Bibliography

I. Books containing background for, and/or varied insights into the Synoptic Gospels.

Ahern, B., New Horizons (Notre Dame, Ind.: Fides Publishers, 1963).

Anderson, H. and Barclay, W., The New Testament in Historical and Contemporary Perspective (Oxford, England: Blackwell, 1965).

Bea, A., The Study of the Synoptic Gospels (New York: Harper and Row, 1965).

Bonsirven, J., Palestinian Judaism in the Time of Christ (New York: Holt, Rinehart, Winston, 1964).

———— Theology of the New Testament (Westminster, Md.: Newman, 1963).

Bornkamm, G., et al., Tradition and Interpretation in Matthew (Philadelphia: Westminster Press, 1963).

Bright, J., The Kingdom of God (New York: Abingdon, 1953).

Bultmann, R., The History of the Synoptic Tradition (New York: Harper and Row, 1963).

———— Primitive Christianity in its Contemporary Setting (New York: Meridian Books, 1956).

———— Theology of the New Testament (New York: Scribners, 1951).

Charles, R., Eschatology, Doctrine of a Future Life in Israel, Judaism and Christianity (New York: Schocken, 1963).

Conzelmann, H., The Theology of St. Luke (New York: Harper and Row, 1961).

Cullmann, O., Christ and Time (Philadelphia: Westminster Press, 1964).

———— Christology of the New Testament (Philadelphia: Westminster Press, 1957).

Danielou, J., Theology of Jewish Christianity (Chicago: H. Regnery, 1964).

Davis, W. and Daube, D., The Background of the New Testament and its Eschatology (New York: Cambridge University Press, 1964).

Dodd, C., *The Apostolic Preaching and its Developments* (New York: Harper and Row, 1951).
—— *Christ and the New Humanity* (Bronxville, N. Y.: Cambridge University Press, 1965).
—— *The Old Testament in the New* (Philadelphia: Fortress Press, 1964).
—— *The Parables of the Kingdom* (New York: Scribners, 1961).
Durwell, F., *The Resurrection, A Biblical Study* (New York: Sheed and Ward, 1960).
Filson, F., *A New Testament History* (Philadelphia: Westminster Press, 1964).
Finklestein, L., *The Pharisees, The Sociological Background of Their Faith* (Philadelphia: Jewish Publication Society, 1962).
Fuller, R., *The Foundations of New Testament Christology* (New York: Scribner, 1965).
Glen, J., *Parables of Conflict in Luke* (Philadelphia: Westminster Press, 1952).
Grant, F., *Introduction to New Testament Thought* (New York: Abingdon, 1964).
Gutzwiller, R., *The Parables of the Lord* (New York: Herder and Herder, 1964).
Harrington, W., *Record of the Fulfillment: The New Testament* (Dubuque, Iowa: Priory Press, 1960).
—— *Key to the Parables* (Glen Rock, N. J.: Paulist Press, 1964).
Harrison, R., *Archaeology of the New Testament* (New York: Association Press, 1964).
Hartdegen, S., *A Chronological Harmony of the Gospels* (Paterson, N. J.: St. Anthony Guild Press, 1948).
Hartman, L., *Encyclopedic Dictionary of the Bible* (New York: McGraw-Hill, 1963).
Hermann, I., *Encounter With The New Testament: An Initiation* (New York: P. J. Kenedy and Sons, 1965).
Hopkins, M., *God's Kingdom in the New Testament* (Chicago: H. Regnery, 1965).
Hunt, I., *Understanding the Bible* (New York: Sheed and Ward, 1962).
Hunter, A., *Introducing New Testament Theology* (Philadelphia: Westminster Press, 1957).
Jeremias, J., *The Central Message of the New Testament* (New York: Scribner's, 1965).
—— *The Parables of Jesus* (New York: Scribner's, 1963).
Jocz, J., *The Jewish People and Jesus Christ* (London: S.P.C.K., 1949).
Jones, A., *God's Living Word* (New York: Sheed and Ward, 1961).
Kee, H. et al., *Understanding the New Testament* (Englewood Cliffs, N. J.: Prentice-Hall, 1965).

Kittel, G. and Bromiley, G., *Theological Dictionary of the New Testament* (Grand Rapids: Eerdmann's, 1964).

Klausner, J., *The Messianic Idea in Israel* (London: Allen and Unwin, 1956).

Leslie, R., *Jesus and Logotherapy* (New York: Abingdon, 1965).

McKenzie, J., *Authority in the Church* (New York: Sheed and Ward, 1966).

———— *Dictionary of the Bible* (Milwaukee: Bruce, 1965).

———— *The Power and the Wisdom* (Milwaukee: Bruce, 1965).

Malevez, L., *The Christian Message and Myth* (Westminster, Md.: Newman, 1960).

Manson, T., *The Servant-Messiah* (New York: Cambridge University Press, 1961).

Moule, C., *Studies in Biblical Theology* (London/Naperville, Ill.: SCM Press/Alec R. Allenson, Inc.). Monographs of New Testament interests.

Moulton, R., *The Modern Reader's Bible* (New York: Macmillan Co., 1952).

Mowinckel, S., *He That Cometh* (New York: Abingdon, 1954).

Mowry, L., *Dead Sea Scrolls and Early Church* (Chicago: University of Chicago Press, 1962).

Paupert, *What is the Gospel* (Hawthorn Encyclopedia, # 69, 1962).

Quesnell, Q., *This Good News* (Milwaukee: Bruce, 1964).

Rollins, W., *Gospels, Portraits of Christ* (Philadelphia: Westminster, 1963).

Reicke, B., *The Gospel of Luke* (Richmond, Va.: John Knox Press, 1964).

Richardson, A., *An Introduction to the Theology of the New Testament* (New York: Harper and Row, 1958).

Robert, A. and Feuillet, A., *Introduction to the New Testament* New York: Desclée, 1965).

Ryan, R., *Contemporary New Testament Studies* (Collegeville, Minn.: Liturgical Press, 1965).

Schnackenburg, R., *The Church in the New Testament* (New York: Herder and Herder, 1965).

———— *God's Rule and Kingdom* (New York: Herder and Herder, 1963).

———— *The Moral Teaching of the New Testament* (New York: Herder and Herder, 1965).

———— *New Testament Theology* (New York: Herder and Herder, 1963).

Schurer, E., *A History of the Jewish People in the Time of Jesus* (New York: Schocken Books, 1961).

Short, R., *The Gospel According to Peanuts* (Richmond, Va.: John Knox Press, 1964).

Stanley, D., *The Apostolic Church in the New Testament* (Westminster, Md.: Newman, 1965).

Stauffer, E., _Jesus and the Wilderness Community at Qumran_ (Phila-delphia: Fortress Press, 1964).

Steinmann, J., _Biblical Criticism_ (New York: Hawthorn's Encyclo-pedia, # 63, 1958).

Taylor, V., _The Gospels_, 9th ed. (London, Epworth Press, 1960).

Thurneysen, E., _The Sermon on the Mount_ (Richmond, Va.: John Knox Press, 1964).

Vawter, Bruce, _The Four Gospels: An Introduction_ (New York: Doubleday, 1967).

Wikenhauser, A., _New Testament Introduction_ (New York: Herder and Herder, 1958).

II. Books on the Life of Christ or the Quest for the Historical Jesus.

Amiot, F., _Sources for Life of Christ_ (New York: Hawthorn's En-cyclopedia, No. 67, 1962).

Anderson, H., _Jesus and Christian Origins_ (New York: Oxford Uni-versity Press, 1964).

Bornkamm, G., _Jesus of Nazareth_ (New York: Harper and Row, 1960).

Bultmann, R., _History and Eschatology_ (New York: Harper Torch-books, 1955).

——— _Jesus Christ and Mythology_ (New York: Scribner's, 1958).

——— _Jesus and the Word_ (New York: Scribner's, 1958).

——— _Kerygma and Myth_ (New York: Harper Torchbooks, 1953).

Dodd, C., _History and the Gospels_ (Welwyn, England: Nisbet, 1938).

Dulles, A., _Apologetics and the Biblical Christ_ (Westminster, Md.: Newman, 1963).

Fernandez, A., _The Life of Christ_ (Westminster, Md.: Newman, 1959).

Fuchs, E., _Studies of the Historical Jesus_ (London/Naperville, Ill.: SCM, Allenson, 1960).

Grant, R., _Historical Introduction to the New Testament_ (New York: Harper and Row, 1960).

Guardini, R., _The Humanity of Christ_ (New York: Pantheon, 1963).

Henderson, J., _Myth in the New Testament_ (London/Naperville, Ill.: SCM, Allenson, 1952).

Jeremias, J., _The Problem of the Historical Jesus_ (Philadelphia: Fortress Press, 1964).

Kahler, M., _The So-Called Historical Jesus and the Historic Biblical Christ_ (Philadelphia: Fortress Press, 1964).

Lagrange, M. J., _Jesus Christ_ (Westminster, Md.: Newman, 1938).

McGinley, L., _Form-Criticism of the Synoptic Healing Narrative_ (Woodstock, Md.: Woodstock College Press, 1944).

Prat, F., *Jesus Christ* (Milwaukee: Bruce, 1950).

Ricciotti, G., *The Life of Christ* (Milwaukee: Bruce, 1947).

Robinson, J., *New Quest of the Historical Jesus* (London/Naperville, Ill.: SCM, Allenson, 1959).

Robinson, J. A. T., *Honest to God* (Philadelphia: Westminster, 1961).

Robinson, J. A. T. and Edwards, D., *The Honest to God Debate* (London: SCM Press, 1963).

Ruef, John S., *The Gospels and the Teachings of Jesus: An Introduction for Laymen* (New York: The Seabury Press, 1967).

Schweitzer, A., *Quest of the Historical Jesus* (New York: Macmillan, 1961).

Steinmann, J., *The Life of Jesus* (Boston: Little, Brown, and Co., 1963).

Taylor, V., *Formation of the Gospel Tradition* (New York: St. Martin's, 1960).

———— *Life and Ministry of Jesus* (New York: Abingdon Press, 1955).

———— *Names of Jesus* (New York: St. Martin's, 1961).

———— *Person of Christ in New Testament Teaching* (New York: St. Martin's, 1959).

Vawter, B., *The Four Gospels* (Huntington, Ind.: Our Sunday Visitor Press, 1958).

Zahrnt, H., *The Historical Jesus* (New York: Harper and Row, 1960).

Scriptural Index

Subject Index

Abandonment of Jesus, 33

Abba, definition of, 30; a liturgical expression, 30

Abraham, Jesus' fulfillment of promises to, 40; Zacchaeus, true son of, 112

Abyss, 20

Acts, authorship, 81; date of, 82; expansion of Gospel, 86; "we-passages," 81

Adultery, Jesus' teachings on, 23; Mary and, 46; Old Testament on, 45

Allegorical parable, 62 n, 103

Allegory, definition of, 62; different from parable, 78; of forgiveness and Roman world, 71; limitless forgiveness, 69

Anawim, Mk's definition, 26

Angel, God's messenger, 69

Angel of the Lord, 46, 47

Annunciation, Jesus', 90 f; John the Baptist's, 90; Lk, 91

Anointed, see Messiah

Antinomians, approach to life, 49

Apocalypse, details of, 75; history of, 75

Apocalyptic, Gehenna and, 59

Appetites, happiness and, 52

Aquinas, St. Thomas, 51; beatitudes and, 52

Ark of Covenant, Mary as the personification of, 97

Ashre, 51

Assisi, Francis, and Luke, 82

Assumption of Moses, 74

Awe, Jesus and, 21; in Mk, 7, 20, 21, 28

Bakar, 51

Baptism, early Church on child, 25

Beatitudes, 48; kingdom of heaven and, 26; reality and, 51

Beelzebub, explanation of, 57 f

"Before," meaning in relationship of Mary and Joseph, 47

Betrayal, of Jesus, 27, 30, 31

Birth, of Jesus, 90; of John the Baptist, 90

Blessed, meaning of, 51

Blessing, Jesus to children, 26

Body, 59

Brotherhood, true, 69

Cain, 70

Cenacle, 27

Charity, see Love

Children, Jesus and, 24; Mk and, 18; Roman law and, 26

"Children of," Semitism for "Nature of," 107

Christ, as "the whole Christ," 11; see also Messiah or Jesus or Savior

Christian, sin and, 69; value of, 69

Christology, Mk and development of, 12

Church, Israel and, 64; of Jesus, 41; official interpretation of, x; parables in Mt and, 64; and the transmission of Christ's life and words, vi

Circumcision, salvation and, 87

Clement of Alexandria, and authorship of Lk, 81; and authorship of Mk, 1; and date of Mk, 2

Coin, the lost, 86, 104

Comfort, for the sorrowing, 54

Commission, manager's right to, 107

Comparison, as literary form, 62, 65

Confidence, 94; Lk on, 85

Consciousness, human, definition of, 13; divine, and Jesus, 12, 31; Jesus' human, and knowledge of parousia, 77

Contemplation, happiness and, 52

Cosmogony, Jewish, 10

Covenant, Ark of, 97; Eucharist, 27; Old, and its reward, 53

Creation, see Supercreation

Cup, biblical definition of, 30; of Jesus, 31

Daughter of Zion, fear and, 95; Mary as personification of, 92

David, 42, 43; Jesus as son of, 96; as Joseph's father, 45

Davidic-King, title of Jesus, 91

Day of the Lord, Jesus' knowledge of, 77; kingdom of God and, 25

Death, and inheritance, 103; of Jesus, 27, 33; Lord of, 20; salvation from, 86; Sheol and, 20

Dedication, happiness of in Mt, 67

126

Subject Index

Deluge, see Flood
Denarii, its approximate worth, 72
Devils, salvation from, 86
Disciple, attitude of toward the Sabbath, 102; attitude of toward self-sufficiency, 102; crucifixion and, 50; devil's, 58; and learning from the worldly wise, 107; response of Mammon, 109; qualities of in Lk, 102; qualities of in Mt, 64; scandal of, 27; see also Christian and Missionary
Divorce, Mt and, 41
Divinity, Jesus and his consciousness of, 12, 31
Docetism, Mk and, 23
Dove, 10, 11
Dream, God's witness, 46

Ego eimi, 22
Egypt, flight from, 42
Ekron, 57
Elizabeth, 98
Emmanuel, 40, 46, 48; dying, 72; happiness and, 67; king, 57; meaning of, 47
Enoch, Book of, 74
Ephraim, 43
Eschatology, hour and, 30; Kingdom of God and, 25; Mark and, 8, 10; marriage and, 78; parables and, 64; see Parousia
Essences, 16
Eternity, punishment and, 59
Eucharist, Mark and, 18; sacrifice, 27
Eusebius of Caesarea, and the authorship of Mt, 36
Evil, punishment of, 59
Example story, definition of, 110; literary form of, 77, 78; and Zacchaeus, 110
Existentialism, happiness and, 51; Mark and, 118

Faith, ideal of piety, 21; in Mark, 7, 18
Faith, perserverance in asking for, 110; as a quality of a disciple in Mt, 64
Fasting, Jesus' teaching on, vii, 14
Fear, definition of in Mk, 21; in Mk, 7, 20; early Church and, 95; God and, 59; Jesus and, 21; and Mary, 95; self-reliance and, 101
Family, qualities of Christian, 68
Fear of God, forgiveness and, 72
Feet, washing of, 100
Flesh, definition of, 30
Flood, historicity of and Mt, 78

Forgiveness, God's, 54, 68, 72, 100, 170; God's and Christians', 54, 68, 69, 70, 72, 100
Franckl, Victor E., 52

Gabriel, 89; etymology, 92; Mark and, 26, 93; Mary's Virginity and, 96
Gehenna, definition of, 59
Genealogy, of Jesus, 44
Gentiles, as the audience of Lk and Acts, 82
Gethsemani, 28; Jesus in, 22; Jesus and the will of God in, 30; Jesus' prayer in, 31; Jesus' sorrows in, 28
Glory, as a title of Jesus, 91, 95
God, the world and, 106
"God with us," Jesus as, 44; see Emmanuel
Golden Rule, 49
"Good" Person, 105
Good Samaritan, 86; as an example-story, 110
Gospel, and literary form, 3, 37
Gospel of Luke, see Luke, Gospel of
Gospel of Mark, see Mark, Gospel of
Gospel of Peter, 1
Gospels, as Christ's life and words, viii; history and, vi, xi; literary forms in, x; oral sources of, ix; and principles of interpretation, ix; as three levels of tradition, v; verses identical in, ix; and written sources, ix

"Hail Mary," 93
Happiness, appetite and, 52; beatitudes and, 51, 58; correct notion of 52; in Mt, 79; ontological definition of, 51; parable of buried treasure and, 67; parable of great pearl and, 67; peace and, 55; psychological meaning of, 52; suffering and, 50; wealth and, 52
Hardness of heart, 23, 63, 64; definition of, 16
Heavens, Mk and, 12; opening of, 10
Hell, 59
Hellenistic faction in early church, 87
Hemorrhage, woman with, 21
Herod, Antipas, 17; Jesus and, 43; John and, 21; Pharisees and, 17
Herodians, 16
History, definition of, xi; Mk and, 17
Holiness, dedication to, 106; hunger and thirst for, 54; Jesus', increase in, 22; Joseph and, 45; meaning